What People Are Saying about Richard Farson's Management of the Absurd

"Fabulous! This may be the best book on leadership I've ever read. It annoys, irritates, goads . . . and inevitably leads you to question things you should have questioned decades before. 'How to' it isn't. Instead it is genuinely wise."
—Tom Peters

"*Management of the Absurd* knocks some cherished management ideas right on their silly butts, no easy accomplishment. Farson is a very smart and original thinker and well worth listening to."
—Richard Carlson
CEO, Corporation for Public Broadcasting

"*Management of the Absurd* is a delightfully irreverent book that addresses the real truths of management at an interpersonal level. After reading it, I felt as if I had just emerged from a cold shower—a bit shocked, refreshed, and feeling a bit better about myself."
—David T. McLaughlin
Chairman, The Aspen Institute
former President, Dartmouth College

"Over the years, one thing about Richard Farson has become increasingly clear: Ideas of his that at first seem contrarian and far-fetched have a tenacious way of working themselves into the mainstream. The business community would be wise to heed his message in *Management of the Absurd*."
—Richard Pollack
Editor-at-Large, The Nation

"Farson's insight into the behavior of managers is truly extraordinary. By exposing the absurdities of fashions in management style, he offers hope that leaders may yet back off, reexamine their assumptions, and become more effective."
—Raymond M. Alden
Retired President, United Telecom

"Unconventional wisdom from a remarkable thinker! This is the kind of book that makes you run out and buy copies for all your friends."
—Rachel McCulloch
Rosen Family Professor of Economics
Brandeis University

"Richard Farson's unconventional thinking never fails to surprise, and he's done it again with *Management of the Absurd*. I can imagine that Japanese executives will be jolted by reading this book, and may scratch their heads for a while, but in the end will be richly rewarded by his refreshing and valuable insights."
—Masami Shigeta
President, AMSECO International, Inc.

"Managers place their faith in certain documents that give them confidence to face the irrational and succeed. To that list can now be added *Management of the Absurd*. This book is chock-full of ideas that will make 'in-a-rut' managers have second thoughts. Simply reading the chapter headings is worth the price of the book."
—Bill Lacy
President, Purchase College, SUNY

"*Management of the Absurd* incorporates more wisdom about management than any book I have ever read. It is destined to become a classic in the field."
—Michael Murphy
Founder and Chairman, Esalen Institute

"Richard Farson has written a wise and wonderful counterfoil to simplistic solutions to complex problems."
—Sandy Mactaggert
Chairman, Maclab Enterprises
Former Chancellor, University of Alberta, Canada

"Richard Farson articulates the paradoxes of leadership and management with insight, grace, and remarkable honesty. These ideas will not only change your perspective on organizations but also deepen your understanding of human relationships. It is a very important work."
—Mary E. Boone
Author of *Leadership and the Computer*

"In this book, Dr. Farson takes us on a safari through the jungles of accepted management nostrums and the savannas of organizational bromides. He challenges some long-accepted concepts as mythical and sometimes dangerous beasts. He brings into focus the real dilemmas, predicaments, and paradoxes of that puzzle that frustrates all of us in our personal and business lives as we try to fulfill creative leadership roles."
—Douglas Strain
Founding Chairman, Electro Scientific Industries

"The absurdities of conventional management wisdom pile up in this wise, comforting, and heartening book."
—Mary Douglas
Former Professor of Social Anthropology
University of London
Author, *How Institutions Think*

"Good designers have always embraced the absurd. Finally, an author asks managers to do the same. It doesn't matter whether Richard Farson's delightful paradoxes always work. Like Talmudic riddles, they spin you around and you're the wiser for the ride."
—Julian Beinart
Professor of Architecture, MIT

"Wise, witty, and wonderfully wry."
—Charles Hampden-Turner
Author of *Seven Cultures of Capitalism*

"Farson has written a succinct and charming book on the nuances of leadership. Stands out from the usual homilies about how to be a manager —a work of humanity and wisdom."
—Robert Kuttner
Editor, *The American Prospect*
Economics Columnist, *Business Week*

"Reading Dr. Farson's provocative book is a lot like talking with him: you enjoy it. Even when you disagree, you feel stimulated, entertained, enlightened, and amused—and you benefit from each minute you get to spend with this special man."
—Spencer Johnson, M.D.
Originator, co-author, *The One Minute Manager*

"I first encountered Dick Farson's unique management perspective at the Western Behavioral Sciences Institute, where a group of experimental corporate leaders assembled to learn more about electronic-enhanced meetings, group linkages, and (though we didn't know it) management dilemmas. Many of us thought that e-mail was the message, and in 1982, that was quite a message. But the management and strategic impact lore, and the deeply counterintuitive behavioral outlook that Dick conveyed, through one example after another, was the real message. I have seldom encountered such a thinker, or teacher, certainly not in the management consultant profession, or at the business schools.

His impact on these students, who included a number of America's budding corporate leaders, had consequential influence on such companies as Hewlett-Packard, Levi-Strauss, Tektronix, and Digital Equipment. It is very satisfying, finally, to find his thoughts and concepts in print, so that a much wider audience can come to appreciate his profound thinking, observation, and point of view."

—Charles House
Executive Vice President and General Manager
Centerline Software

Management
of the Absurd

PARADOXES IN LEADERSHIP

by Richard Farson

FOREWORD BY
MICHAEL CRICHTON

SIMON & SCHUSTER
New York • London • Toronto • Sydney • Singapore

SIMON & SCHUSTER
Rockefeller Center
1230 Avenue of the Americas
New York, NY 10020

SIMON & SCHUSTER and colophon are registered trademarks
of Simon & Schuster Inc.

Designed by Irving Perkins Associates, Inc.

Manufactured in the United States of America

1 3 5 7 9 10 8 6 4 2

Library of Congress Cataloging-in-Publication Data
Farson, Richard Evans, date.
Management of the absurd : paradoxes in
leadership / by Richard Farson ; foreword by Michael Crichton.
p. cm.
ISBN 0-684-80080-2
1. Management. 2. Leadership. I. Title.
HD31.F273   1996
658.4—dc20   95-25346
CIP

Contents

Foreword

THE CHALLENGING BOOK you are holding in your hands was written by a remarkable man. Richard Farson has been my friend for many years, and his way of thinking is so unusual that you may want to know a little about him before you start. In person, he is tall, distinguished, gray-haired, and always ready to laugh. Everybody I know loves him. He is one of the warmest, kindest, and most intriguing men I have ever met.

At the same time, his unusual way of thinking sometimes gives people difficulties. Dick developed his ideas over many decades while working at a wide range of jobs—academic psychologist, naval officer, college dean, CEO, and management consultant. And in the process, he long ago became comfortable with the fact that people may greet his counterintuitive views with some mixture of anger and disbelief.

I've watched him give lectures that produced the most remarkable combination of feelings in his audiences. Dick is so personable and so genuinely human that he's enormously likable—he's a good walking advertisement for his own philosophy. Yet his message makes people squirm.

In his easygoing, anecdotal way, he emphasizes the inevitability of unintended outcomes, paradoxical consequences, and unknowable realities in human affairs. At bottom, his message is humane and warm, but for any group that believes some variant of the idea that knowledge is power,

Dick's thesis is hard to hear, even exasperating. It takes a while for people to calm down long enough to even consider it.

I've struggled with certain of his ideas for years. Once he said to me that he felt people don't learn from their mistakes, only from their successes. Instinctively I disagreed, but by then I knew him well enough to realize that I might be on shaky ground. I turned this idea around in my mind for a long time, examining my own behavior and the behavior of the groups I was involved in. I finally decided that Farson was correct for group behavior, but not necessarily for individuals—at least, not for me. I'm much more likely to make a radical change after a personal failure; I will make no change at all after success. And in a group failure, the responsibility is so disseminated, the reason so uncertain, I never feel any need to change.

Earlier this year, after a particularly disturbing, wrenching work encounter that I judged to be a failure, I found myself walking on the beach, plotting the steps I would take so that this would never happen again. As I considered it, I realized my plan amounted to a rather large change in the way I operated. But the failure had energized me to make a change that was probably long overdue. At the end I nearly shouted, "Dick, you're wrong!"

I'm sure he'd just laugh, and wait for me to think it through again. And certainly it is a tribute to the power of his way of looking at things, that gnawing, irritating sense that maybe he's right after all, which has made me consider his ideas in a sustained way for so long.

As I read his new book, I often found myself thinking, "No, no, no!" or sometimes, "Oh, come on!" He irritated me. He provoked me. He made me nod, he made me smile, and he made me shake my head. In this book Richard Farson reports more than experience; he gives us something I would call wisdom. Now you can be stimulated, intrigued, amused, and exasperated too.

—Michael Crichton

Introduction

Embracing Paradox and Absurdity

There is only one truth, steadfast, healing,
salutary, and that is the absurd.
— ANDREW SALMON

ALL OF US like to think that human affairs are essentially rational, that they work like other things in our world, and that we should therefore be able to make them work for us. The wealth of experience that fails to support this notion never seems to faze us. Small wonder, then, that it may require some effort to accept the ideas presented in this book —that life is absurd, that human affairs usually work not rationally but paradoxically, and that (fortunately) we can never quite master our relationships with others.

That is certainly true in regard to our relationships in business and other bureaucratic organizations. It is my hope to encourage managers and all those in positions of leadership to think beyond the conventional wisdom—in particular, to understand how the ways we think shape what we see, and how paradox and absurdity inevitably play a part in our every action.

I am inspired, of course, by that group of post–World War II playwrights—Pinter, Ionesco, Genet, Beckett, and others —who questioned the assumptions of traditional theater, criticizing it for oversimplifying and overrationalizing human affairs. They felt that only by recognizing the mystery and absurdity of life was the dignity of the human being served. Collectively, their work became known as the "Theater of the Absurd," and it turned out to be an important moment in the history of dramatic art. I believe that we need such a moment now in regard to the art of management.

The Wrong Direction

Examining the absurd is not just a playful exercise. I believe that many programs in management training today are moving us in the wrong direction because they fail to appreciate the complexity and paradoxical nature of human organizations. Thinking loses out to how-to-do-it formulas and techniques, if not to slogans and homilies, as the principal management guides. I can understand their appeal. Considering the difficulty of the tasks before them, it is not surprising that managers still find themselves prone to accept a definition of management that makes it seem as if it could be simply learned.

Indeed, what's the harm? Why not let managers believe the familiar bromides? As we will see, there is a considerable downside. Leading managers to believe that their responsibilities can be discharged adequately by attending seminars or following simplistic formulas creates just the opposite of its intended effect. When such formulas fail them, managers become frustrated, aggressive, and sometimes verbally abusive.

Still, managers are whipsawed from one fashionable training program to the next as their organizations keep buying into new trends, new definitions of management, new motivational phrases. Years ago we talked about "leadership," then the byword became "morale," then it was "motivation," then "communication," then "culture," then "quality," then "excellence," then "chaos," then back again to "leadership." Along the way we were buffeted about by buzzwords like "zero defect," "management by objectives," "quality circles," "TQM" (total quality management), "paradigm shift," and "re-engineering."

The confused manager, careening from trend to trend, cannot become an effective leader as long as he or she continues to believe in simplistic techniques. But a manager who can appreciate the absurdities and paradoxes of business relationships and organizations is surely going to be far less vulnerable to fashion, and therefore stronger as a leader.

I should note that I use the terms *manager* and *leader* almost interchangeably, even though I know that one can make important distinctions between them. I personally like the one that organization theorist Warren Bennis makes: Managers do things right, leaders do the right things.

Some Definitions

Paradoxes are seeming absurdities. And our natural inclination when confronted with paradoxes is to attempt to resolve them, to create the familiar out of the strange, to rationalize them. In this book, however, we are going to resist that temptation and instead just let them wash over us for a while, to see if we can become comfortable using a kind of paradoxical logic to understand management and human affairs.

The paradoxes in the pages that follow are stated in a deliberately declarative manner, with the full knowledge that they require clarification and qualification. They are meant to challenge conventional ways of thinking and present alternatives to the traditional viewpoints that have been the received wisdom in management literature for many years. All have what I regard as an element of the absurd, and all ask us to turn our thinking upside down. Regard them as exercises for the mind.

Suppose, for example, I were to pose this question: "If you were asked to predict the group in our society that is most likely to mount a liberation effort to end its oppression, would you have a greater probability of success by picking the group for which you feel most sorry, or the one for which you feel least sorry?"

If you employed the unconventional, paradoxical approach, you would have picked the group for which you feel least sorry. Liberation movements usually arise from groups thought at the time to be perfectly content. That is why they so often have taken society by surprise. Earlier generations, for example, complacently saw Negroes as being happy in their place. Women, before the 1960s, were thought to be on a pedestal, adored and provided for by men. And today, in spite of the efforts of child advocates to call attention to the often oppressive conditions of childhood, children remain in the public mind as carefree, fully protected, joyful in their innocence.

Next question: "From where is the leadership of those liberation movements most likely to come—from those most oppressed by the conditions or those least oppressed?"

If you said least oppressed, you're beginning to get the idea. The leaders come from outside or from the margins of these groups, seldom from the most oppressed segments. African-Americans were most helped at first by white abolitionists. Gloria Steinem is hardly the most oppressed woman in America. Children are represented almost entirely by adult advocates.

As we explore the paradoxes of management, keep in mind that there is a difference between absurdity and stupidity. Stupidity is behavior that can be recognized to be mistaken, incompetent, or blind to the facts. It refers to insensibility, not having all of one's faculties available. With stupid management, it is easy for someone else to see how to do it right. Absurdity, on the other hand, arises from the essential humanness of the situation. Absurd behavior jars us. It seems unreasonable, even ridiculous. It is not what we would expect a rational person to do. It contradicts our conventional ways of thinking and it usually confronts us not with a problem, but with a dilemma. Even the best of us are not sure what to do.

Paradox and absurdity keep us off balance. In so doing, they produce the humility, vitality, and creative surprise that make life so worth living. But they cannot be controlled. They will always defy the attempt.

I find it disquieting to see the term *paradox* entering management literature in a way that indicates it can be "managed." I suppose we should expect this because of the sense of omnipotence that plagues American management, the belief that no event or situation is too complex or too unpredictable to be brought under management control.

But as Charles Handy points out in his book *The Age of Paradox*, "Paradox can only be 'managed' in the sense of coping with, which is what *management* had always meant until the term was purloined to mean planning and control." Thus, paradox is not just another organizational factor to be brought into the workshop of the management technologist. It would be misleading even to suggest that it can be coped with in any systematic or rational way. It will never be that comfortable. Therefore, as you will no doubt discern in the pages that follow, the phrase "management of the absurd" is, itself, an absurdity.

In Pursuit of the Paradoxical

My contrarian view of human relations and my interest in paradoxical thinking have been with me so long that I'm not sure when or where they began. Certainly, I have profited from having worked closely with the late and distinguished psychologist Carl Rogers, as his student, his research assistant, and his colleague at the University of Chicago, and eventually as president of the Western Behavioral Sciences Institute, where he did some of his most important work. Over the years I watched him take positions that were in striking contrast to the mainstream thinking of the day, defend them successfully, and eventually see them incorporated so thoroughly into the mainstream that most people now don't even know where the ideas came from. He has been called America's most influential psychologist, and he certainly provided an example of how one should think for oneself, questioning the conventional wisdom.

My long friendship with the exceptionally creative social psychologist Alex Bavelas, who is a major contributor to our understanding of organizations, surely aided my pursuit of the paradoxical. I was a junior member of the human relations faculty at the Harvard Business School (he was then a professor at nearby MIT) when I first encountered him face-to-face and experienced his remarkable ability to take a completely fresh look at ideas, often turning them upside down, illuminating the paradoxes.

There were other influences. I worked at universities, research institutes, and as a naval officer, studying leadership and organizational behavior. I consulted with corporations, government agencies, and nonprofit organizations. But probably the most important contribution to my thinking has been my thirty-plus years heading organizations. Being both a psychologist and a CEO has given me a special appreciation of the paradoxes and absurdities of organizations, and how nothing works quite the way we have been taught.

I could honestly title this book *What I Wish I Had Known Forty Years Ago*. It is a book of ideas, observations, and lessons learned, not a book of management techniques. I have organized it first to delve into the nature of paradoxical thinking, then to examine particular paradoxes that we all encounter in human relationships and organizations. Along the way, I will call attention to those qualities of effective leadership that often go unrecognized.

These chapters need not necessarily be read in sequence, but can be read in whatever order appeals to the reader. It is my hope that they will strike familiar notes in the reader's own experience, and in so doing will lead to the development of a more realistic way of assessing situations, a more fully integrated approach to managing oneself and others, a more genuine and potent leadership style, and an improved ability to contribute to the success of organizations at whatever managerial level one works.

I know from having talked with hundreds of managers that the ideas in this book can be disturbing initially. But I also know that after managers have enough exposure to them, it is possible not only to entertain these ideas, but also to take comfort in them. After all, the beauty of paradoxical thinking in management is its timelessness. Most ideas come and go with discouraging regularity in management literature and executive training programs. But paradox and absurdity will be with us as long as humans congregate in organizations.

PART ONE

A Different Way
of Thinking

1

The Opposite of a Profound Truth
Is Also True

OUR GREAT ACHIEVEMENTS in science, law, government, and
in every intellectual pursuit are dependent upon our development as rational, logical thinkers.

But this kind of thinking has also limited us. Without quite
knowing it, we have become creatures of linear, categorical
logic. Things are good or bad, true or false, but not both.
We have been taught that a thing cannot be what it is and
also its opposite. Yet it sounds wise when confronted with a
conflict to say, "Well, yes and no." Or, "It's both." We've
all heard statements that concede the coexistence of opposites: Less is more. Living is dying. Hating is loving. Although
it seems illogical, no two things are as closely related as
opposites.

Going in Both Directions

What practical value can we get out of that notion? At a
mundane level, take, for example, the development of frozen food processing. It led to a rash of predictions about
the growth of a fast-food market—predictions that certainly
turned out to be correct. What was not predicted, however,
was the popularity of gourmet cookbooks, with their empha-

sis on fresh ingredients, organically grown products, wholesome preparation, and a new respect for chefs. Frozen food processing made possible the development of fast food, but along with that development came its opposite.

We have seen the coexistence of opposites in management with the introduction of participative approaches designed to democratize the workplace. These approaches often do increase worker participation. But it is also true that hierarchy and authority remain very much in place, perhaps stronger than ever. That is because the executives who grant the work force some amount of authority never lose any of their own authority. Granting authority is not like handing out a piece of pie, wherein you lose what you give away. It is more like what happens when you give information to someone. Although he or she may now know more, you do not know any less.

Practical Deceptions

Another coexistence of opposites: To be healthy, an organization needs full and accurate communication among its members. But also, to be healthy, it needs distortion and deception. If those words sound overly harsh, think of commonly used terms like *diplomacy* and *tact,* which imply less than candid communication.

Just as the profession of medicine or the conduct of a romance requires mystique—that is, encouraging beliefs about oneself that may not be completely accurate but make others feel positively—so, too, do leadership and management. Some, for example, hold that one function of middle management is to massage or filter information, both upward and downward. Such "distortion" or "deception" is said to serve two practical purposes.

First, workers are led to believe that their leaders are confident, fair, and capable, reinforcing the necessary myths of leadership. Second, since the top leaders surely would be

troubled by knowing everything that goes on in the organization, they are protected from hearing about the petty problems and minor failures of the work force.

In human affairs, some form of deception is the rule, not
the exception. In most cases it should not be considered
lying, because that term fails to take into account the complexity of human communication and the many ways people
must maneuver to keep relationships on an even keel. Appreciating the coexistence of opposites helps us understand
that honesty and deception can function together in some
paradoxical way.

Contradictory Impulses

One executive I know is a classic example of a man who
wants to succeed but at the same time seems to want to fail.
Everything he does carries both messages. From the very
moment he enthusiastically volunteers to head a project, he
operates in such a way as to cripple it—refusing to delegate,
undermining the work of committees, failing to meet dead-
lines, and stalling on crucial decisions.

His behavior is not that unusual. Contradictory impulses
to both succeed and fail can be found in every project, every
work team, even every individual. Every management choice,
job offer, or new applicant can appear both appealing and
unappealing. Every deal is both good and bad. That is why
leadership is essentially the management of dilemmas, why
tolerance for ambiguity—coping with contradictions—is essential for leaders, and why appreciating the coexistence of
opposites is crucial to the development of a different way of
thinking.

Like One

There is yet another spin to this paradox that I have always
found intriguing—that opposites not only can coexist, but

can even *enhance* one another. Take pleasure and pain, for example. Scratching an itch is both. Not pleasure, then pain, or pain, then pleasure, but both at once. Granted, scratching an itch too long can become very painful and no longer pleasurable, but there is a moment when they coexist, when they are one. Like truth and falsity, good and evil.

2

Nothing Is as Invisible
as the Obvious

THE MOST IMPORTANT discoveries, the greatest art, and the best management decisions come from taking a fresh look at what people take for granted or cannot see precisely because it is too obvious. I call this the "invisible obvious." Consider these examples.

• James Watt started the industrial revolution with the simple observation of the power of steam escaping from his teakettle. It led to the invention of the steam engine. But to millions of others who had seen the same homely phenomenon, that possible new source of power was invisible.

• Researchers had long observed that penicillium mold inhibited the growth of bacteria on an agar plate. But it took Alexander Fleming to realize that the mold might also inhibit the growth of microorganisms in the body. His observation, of course, led to the development of antibiotics.

• From their beginnings in the nineteenth century and for many years thereafter, automobiles were manufactured individually by teams of multiskilled craftsmen who were responsible for constructing the whole machine. Henry Ford recognized the invisible obvious: that if workers were assigned only one task and performed it repeatedly, automobiles could be built in a far more efficient manner. That was the beginning of the assembly line, of mass production, and of the new industrial age.

Going to the Source

In the early 1970s, a chain of convenience stores asked the Western Behavioral Sciences Institute to help them reduce store robberies. The stores were not robbed all that often— only about once a year on average, with a typical loss of only one hundred dollars. But the company didn't want its employees to be frightened, and it wanted to avoid the risk of escalation into violence.

For years, the Institute had employed ex-offenders—including several former armed robbers—as research assistants on various of its behavioral science projects. One day the obvious became visible—robbers knew about robbing— and we turned to these ex-offenders as the major resource for our study. They told us why and how they decided to rob a store and what went on in their minds during the robbery. And they interviewed others they knew who had made their living robbing convenience stores. Having studied our findings, the company changed its store designs and a number of its practices, eventually reducing its robberies by 40 percent. The study became a classic in its field.

Now banks and computer companies are hiring hackers to help them develop security systems. Obvious, right?

Looking for Reality

The invisible obvious is a major factor in why the prediction of future trends is especially difficult. Naturally, such predictions rely heavily on knowledge of present conditions. But present conditions are largely invisible, even to those who spend their lives looking at them.

In 1967, two of our most respected futurists, Herman Kahn and Anthony Wiener, published a book entitled *The Year 2000*. It is a stunningly insightful book, predicting, for example, the emergence of Japan as a major power, the resurgence of religions, and the growth of an exercise industry. But in it there is no mention whatever of energy, pollution, environment, ecology, women's rights—all issues that were then present and were to become highly visible in the public press the very next year, let alone the year 2000. The reality was there to be seen, but even these perceptive observers missed it.

I can remember one instance in which the invisible obvious became dramatically visible to me. In 1966, several years before the modern women's movement clearly emerged, I was a speaker at a conference of two thousand women in New York meeting under the theme "Quo Vadis Today's Woman?" I noticed that all the speakers lined up with me on the stage were men—anthropologist Ashley Montagu, economist Eli Ginsberg, and *Ladies' Home Journal* editor John Mack Carter. It occurred to me then that it would be impossible to imagine that situation in reverse—two thousand men meeting under the theme "Quo Vadis Today's Man?" and listening to four women, no matter how distinguished, tell them where they were going. This striking example of prevailing attitudes about women opened my eyes. What I and the others had all been blind to was, in that moment, painfully obvious.

Discovering the obvious is always a challenge. Analysts who were studying deterrence strategies for the military during the cold war built scenarios based upon expectations that the enemy would respond rationally. Eventually, somebody pointed out what should have been obvious: (1) that even a small weapons system could become a powerful force for one side if the other side thought it would be used; (2) that the more irrational, impulsive, and volatile leaders were more likely to have small weapons systems but also more likely to use them; and (3) the greater the size of the arsenal, the more likely that rational analysis would govern its use and, therefore, the less power it would have.

A Valuable Service

You may have heard the story about a little boy's advice to the authorities who were unable to free an oversized truck that had become wedged under a low bridge. The lad surveyed the situation and then made the sensible (and obvious) suggestion that they could lower the truck by letting some air out of the tires. As the little boy proved, the invisible obvious can be made visible by anyone. It is often the most valuable service one can offer an organization. But it requires nontraditional thinking. Deeply held ideologies and cultural values, tunnel vision, selective perception, deference to the judgment of others—these are all enemies in our efforts to see what is really going on. And when the invisible obvious is pointed out to us, we are likely to have one of two reactions: Either we will reject and ignore it, or, more likely, we will simply say, "Of course!" thinking we surely must have known it all along.

PART TWO

The "Technology" of Human Relations

3

The More Important a Relationship, the Less Skill Matters

AMERICA IS A nation obsessed by technology. We have benefited from so many technological successes that we are now willing, even eager, to apply technology to every area of our lives—even the most personal, such as romance, marriage, and parenthood. When I say that we apply technology in those areas I mean that increasingly we treat human relationships as requiring skill and technique. Thus, it is only natural that we have come to regard the job of a manager as essentially the acquisition of techniques we call "management skills." Hundreds of millions of dollars are spent annually in teaching these skills to managers.

Of course, skills are necessary in management. Gaining skill in planning, organizing, and scheduling no doubt improves the performance of managers. It is when we attempt to apply skills to the most challenging area of management, that of human relations, that they desert us. This is especially true when we try to handle those people who mean the most to us—our closest colleagues. Here, skills don't help.

Answers, but No Method

Perhaps I can illustrate this paradox best by drawing on some examples from parenthood. In a sense parenthood is a special case of management.

Some years ago, to gather material for a book, I talked with a number of adults about their childhood, how they were "parented." One question I asked was: "As you think back over your own childhood and the relationship that you had with your parents, can you remember any specific actions or events which you particularly value and which seem to you to have been significant to your development?" Their responses were charming and often amusing, but it was hard to see how they could be helpful to a new mother or father looking for advice on parenting:

My parents had make-believe fights with wet dishcloths.

When I sat on my dad's lap, he pretended to scold me because my hair tickled his chin.

We loved it when Mom made believe she was Dracula and scared us.

My father, in his coat and tie, sat on the ground with me and ate these dirty baked potatoes I had cooked in the backyard.

We almost died laughing when Daddy fell into our cesspool up to his armpits while playing with us.

When I was learning to drive, I ran into the same car three times, but my mom took the blame.

We really liked it when our parents did their silly monster walk in the supermarket.

The most important feature of these recollections is that they do not represent anything recognizable as a parenting technique or skill. Never, in all my interviews, did anyone ever mention an episode that might have been derived from a parent training manual. For the most part, they spoke of acts that parents did not do deliberately, as something they thought would be good for their children's development. Rather, they remembered acts that had a spontaneous, even accidental quality, sometimes breaking all the rules. These moments were memorable because they were different from what the child was used to getting from the parent. We could construct theories about parental behavior from these responses. But we could not use them to develop techniques or specific "how-to" advice.

I Had to Ask

But what about management? I realized, of course, that the relationship between boss and employee is hardly analogous to a parent-child relationship. But what if I asked people to remember specific incidents with their bosses? Would their responses be in any way similar? Well, I had to find out, so I began to ask everyone I met the same kind of question. You can guess the kind of answers I got.

> While I was taking dictation, my very businesslike boss did something very uncharacteristic. He stopped to kid me about some drops of house paint that I didn't know were in my hair.

> Once when I was drinking after hours with the manager at the restaurant where I worked, he said the only reason he had hired me was to "piss someone off," but I had turned out to be one of the best waiters they ever had.

> I was still learning how to be a paramedic but I felt a lot better when my supervisor confessed that even after thirty years on the job, she still gets very scared at times.

> As a junior faculty member, I had a difficult relationship with the dean of our school until one day when he became emotionally over-wrought and told me how discouraging his career had been. After that, I had a new understanding of him and a much more cooperative attitude.

> My boss and I were so ticked off by management that we applied for jobs together at another company. In the end, we didn't leave, but the experience put a new bond between us.

Not once did any of my respondents cite an episode that could have been learned in a management skill training program. In fact, most recalled behavior that would hardly be thought of as an approved management technique (for example, teasing, losing control emotionally, job hunting with an employee). They tended to be moments that the bosses were not likely to remember and would probably think were insignificant, yet often revealed something of their humanity. In these incidents the bosses may have exhibited spontaneity, genuineness, caring—but not skill.

A Dreadful World Avoided

In both parenthood and management, it's not so much what we *do* as what we *are* that counts. What parents do deliberately appears to make little difference in the most important outcomes—whether their children grow up to be happy or unhappy, successful or unsuccessful, good or evil. There is no question that parents can and should do worthwhile things for their children, but it's what they are that will really matter; for example, whether they are sensitive and caring or cold and indifferent. Most children will adopt the characteristics that define their parents, whether their parents want them to or not.

The same dynamic occurs in management and leadership. People learn—and respond to—what we are. When you stop to think about it, perhaps that is the way it should be. What a dreadful world it would be if we actually did possess the skill to convey something other than what we really are.

4

Once You Find a Management Technique That Works, Give It Up

EACH NEW HUMAN relations technique always promises to make the leader more effective. Managers who are taught to listen nonjudgmentally or to reward certain behaviors in others may initially feel that they have found the answer. At last, something that works! But the feeling seldom lasts. Over time, they usually discover that their newfound techniques are actually working to prevent closer human relationships —just the opposite of their intended effect.

The most obvious reason is that any technique loses its power when it becomes evident that it *is* a technique. "Don't listen to me that way." "Don't treat me as if you were my therapist." "I see what you're doing." "Are you rewarding me now?"

As we saw in the previous chapter's examples from parenthood and management, most techniques derive their power from the context in which they are used; that is, they are in contrast to the way things are usually done. If a manager rarely pays attention to an employee and then begins to do so, the effect is quite dramatic. But if the manager is regularly attentive, the attention loses its power because it is not contrasted with its opposite.

Techniques consciously employed to communicate one kind of feeling may be undone by deep-seated and contradictory feelings that are unconsciously transmitted at the same time. The resulting mixed message confuses and disturbs the recipient. It is ineffective to try to send messages that communicate firmness, affection, or interest when opposite feelings are closer to the truth.

An Erosion of Respect

Some managers seem to spend their lives trying to discover techniques that will produce desired behaviors in employees without the employees being aware of them. This is a high-risk approach that will likely end with the managers losing respect for—and confidence in—their employees.

Let me explain. Assume that I have knowledge about certain techniques but my employees lack that knowledge. My compassion for them will almost certainly erode if I succeed in using that knowledge to change their behavior in some way. For they will have been fooled, and I cannot help but lose some respect for them as a result.

The situation is only worsened if I think I *should* be able to "handle" these people, but can't—which, of course, is usually the case. Carl Rogers was perhaps the first to articulate this problem. He knew that when a therapist thought he or she could handle a client, an invisible erosion of respect began. To be truly effective the therapist had to respect the client and be open to whatever might happen.

The same is true in management. It is the ability to meet each situation armed not with a battery of techniques but with openness that permits a genuine response. The better managers *transcend* technique. Having acquired many techniques in their development as professionals, they succeed precisely by leaving technique behind.

Feelings Discovered

One of the most useful ideas to remember is what we might call the "reciprocity rule" of human behavior: that over time, people come to share, reciprocally, similar attitudes toward each other. That is, if I have a low opinion of you, then while you may for a time hold a high opinion of me, it is unlikely that your high opinion will persist. Eventually you will come to feel about me the way I feel about you.

That's another of the snares of the "technology" of human relations. We believe we can acquire techniques that will hide our true feelings about people and enable us to convey an image of ourselves which they will respect, even though we do not respect them. We think, for example, that by learning a communication technique we can gain control over what we are communicating. All this is nothing short of self-deception, I'm afraid. Ultimately, people discover who we are and come to regard us as we regard them. If we genuinely respect our colleagues and employees, those feelings will be communicated without the need for artifice or technique. And they will be reciprocated.

5

Effective Managers Are Not in Control

IF, IN ALL of life, paradox is the rule and not the exception, as I believe it is, then the popular view of management as essentially a matter of gaining and exercising control is badly in need of correction. Management based on techniques of control and manipulation cannot succeed in matters of the absurd. But that hardly means that the manager is lost.

Only those who rely mainly on control are lost.

In my experience, effective leaders and managers do not regard control as the main concern. Instead, they approach situations sometimes as learners, sometimes as teachers, sometimes as both. They turn confusion into understanding. They see a bigger picture. They trust the wisdom of the group. Their strength is not in control alone, but in other qualities—passion, sensitivity, tenacity, patience, courage, firmness, enthusiasm, wonder.

The Vulnerability Requirement

Absurdly, our most important human affairs—marriage, child rearing, education, leadership—do best when there is occasional *loss* of control and an increase in personal vulnerability, times when we do not know what to do.

To explain, let me make clear that I'm not talking about some continuing condition of management passivity or hand-wringing. Nor am I suggesting that managers should fail to act, to exercise their authority or to follow their own good judgment. But people need to know they are dealing with a genuine person, not someone who is "managing" them. Again, it has to do with the inappropriateness of technique.

Think of the difference between seduction and romance. Technique is required for the former but is useless in the latter. Being vulnerable, out of control, buffeted about by the experience, pained at any separation, aching for the next encounter, wild with jealousy, soaring with ecstasy, and plummeting with anxiety— all these are what make it a romance. If you know how to have a romance, it isn't a romance, but a seduction. Not knowing how to do it makes it a romance.

Managers think the people with whom they work want them to exhibit consistency, assertiveness, and self control— and they do, of course. But occasionally, they also want just the opposite. They want a moment with us when we are genuinely ourselves without facade or pretense or defensiveness, when we are revealed as human beings, when we are vulnerable.

This is true not just in leadership but in every human situation. It's what wives want from husbands, what children want from parents, what we all want from each other. It's what most arguments and conflicts are unconsciously designed to produce: to get us to reveal that the other has had an impact on us.

An Idea Misapplied?

Residents of countries outside the United States find rather bewildering the distinctly American idea that the conduct of human relations is basically a matter of finding the right technique. They are amazed and sometimes amused by the self-help psychology books, advice columns, marriage manuals, parent training classes, and motivational videotapes that dominate our popular culture. They think we have misapplied the idea of technology, and have taken it places where it doesn't belong.

Perhaps they are right. It does seem impossible for American managers, and others of us as well, to resist the tendency to translate understanding into technique. When we begin to understand how something works, we think immediately that we will be able to make it work. That may be true in the physical world, but it is far from true in the world of human relations.

Knowing how people grow, for example, does not mean we know how to grow them. Experts in child development are no better than anyone else at raising their own children. Moreover, it should be evident to anyone who is acquainted with psychologists or psychiatrists that knowing about human relationships does not necessarily mean that we are any better at conducting them; indeed, knowing about them may be an impediment.

In some fundamental sense, we cannot learn how to have relationships, how to raise children, how to lead others— how to be human, if you will. Why? Because to a great extent it is the very condition of not knowing, of being vulnerable to and surprised by life, of being unable to manage or control our lovers, our children, or our colleagues, that makes us human.

A Blessing

I used to want to know how to handle my children, my employees, my students, my friends. Now it is a great relief to me to realize that I cannot. Nor, I believe, can anyone else. I especially cannot handle the people I love most: The prospect of such an achievement now appalls me; instead, I think of it as a blessing that I, and we, will never learn.

Many of us have the idea that as managers we can use our skills to shape our employees as if we were shaping clay, molding them into what we want them to become. But that isn't the way it really works. It's more as if our employees are piles of clay into which we fall—leaving an impression, all right, and that impression is distinctly us, but it may not be the impression we intended to leave.

6

Most Problems That People Have Are Not Problems

ONE OF THE most valuable lessons, among many valuable lessons, I learned from philosopher Abraham Kaplan is to distinguish between a problem and a predicament. Problems can be solved; predicaments can only be coped with. Most of the affairs of life, particularly the most intimate and important ones, such as marriage and child rearing, are complicated, inescapable dilemmas—predicaments where no options look very good or better than any other. I believe that is true of management as well.

Not a Simple Matter

A problem is created by something going wrong, by a mistake, defect, disease, or a bad experience. When we find the cause, we can correct it. A predicament, however, paradoxical as it may seem, is more likely to be created by conditions that we highly value. That is why we can only cope with it.

Take crime, for example. We think of crime as a problem and are always looking for its root causes, such as childhood experiences that may have produced a criminal mind. We would prefer it to be a simple matter of cause and effect, so we try to prove that crime comes from such sources as pornography or watching violence on television.

Instead, absurdly, crime exists mainly because of aspects of our society that we wouldn't think of giving up—affluence, urbanization, mobility, freedom, materialism, individual liberty, progress. Social ills such as unemployment and poverty undoubtedly play a part, but there are major societies with poverty far greater than ours that have virtually no crime. In America, as paradoxical as it may sound, crime is associated with developments that we think of as advancement. It even comes from efforts to control it. Prisons, for example, tend to harden and train criminals so that they are likely to commit more serious offenses when they leave. Thus, a predicament is often made worse when we treat it as a problem.

A Larger Frame

Most people, especially those who inhabit the lower levels of organizations, think of themselves as problem solvers, and to a great extent they are. They size up a situation, break it down into its component parts, and then address each component one at a time. As they go up the ladder and become executives, however, they deal increasingly with predicaments, not problems. The best executives soon discover that purely analytic thinking is inadequate.

Predicaments require interpretive thinking. Dealing with a predicament demands the ability to put a larger frame around a situation, to understand it in its many contexts, to appreciate its deeper and often paradoxical causes and consequences. Alas, predicaments cannot be handled smoothly.

7

Technology Creates the Opposite of Its Intended Purpose

THE INTRODUCTION OF the washing machine into the home promised to end the plight of the homemaker who was routinely spending almost an entire day washing clothes. But it also gave rise to the idea of wearing clean clothes on a daily basis. The resulting new standards of cleanliness created a need to wash clothes more often—and the actual number of hours spent at that task remained the same. Similarly, the introduction of the computer to make a paperless office actually increased the amount of paper in offices.

Technology helps us in countless ways, but it always backfires. The term for this phenomenon in medicine is *iatrogenic,* meaning "physician-induced." Examples are complications from surgery, side effects of drugs, infections that result from hospital stays. There are more than a thousand different diseases that would not exist if not for the practice of medicine and the existence of hospitals. Half the time of any hospital staff is spent treating iatrogenic disease.

An Unexpected Counterforce

The problem of backfiring technology is pervasive throughout the sciences. The field of ecology is full of examples in which successful efforts to intervene in the natural course of events on behalf of some species, usually homo sapiens, have produced unexpected damage to that very species, damage which dwarfs the original success.

In Pakistan, for instance, applying the technology of irrigation and fertilization to land that does not drain adequately has had such adverse effects that more land is going out of cultivation than is being brought under cultivation. Closer to home, we have come to see that air-conditioning pollutes the air; widening highways increases congestion not only on the highway but in the cities and towns that it connects; pesticides and preservatives endanger our health.

With every application of technology a counterforce develops that is the exact opposite of what we intended. The danger, of course, is that we become so in love with technological applications that we forget their effect on outcome, so enamored of process that we lose sight of product.

In the world of design, the computer has virtually taken over as a replacement for the art and craft employed by the professional designer. All manner of graphics software is available. Almost any experienced computer operator can create graphic designs similar enough to the designs produced by a professional that the difference does not matter much to the untrained eye.

But, we must ask, is there a missing elegance, humor, and creativity that only a talented designer could have supplied? Are we paying a terrific price for the spread of technology that, while it increases the design capabilities of many more people, actually reduces the opportunity for our most creative designers to apply their skills? Is it possible that the effort to increase design capability will have the backfiring effect of reducing the quality of design?

Hard Questions

The more we encounter the new "gee whiz" technologies, the more often we must ask such questions as: Has the use of magnetic resonance imaging technology in medical diagnostic and treatment procedures improved our health or longevity? Has the introduction of audiovisual technology into schools led to better-educated students? Has computer-aided design, now pervasive in architectural offices, improved architecture? I'm afraid the answers are still no.

The excitement of the new technologies is irresistible—these undreamed-of ways of accomplishing tasks that were previously onerous and arduous. The dilemma, of course, is that it is very difficult to know just in what remote and complex ways they will backfire, but backfire they will.

8

We Think We Invent Technology, but Technology Also Invents Us

THE AUTOMOBILE HAS created not just modern cities but also their opposite, suburbs. What it once made possible—the separation of commercial centers from residential centers from recreational centers from industrial centers—it now makes necessary. The automobile has also become one of the leading causes of injury and death. The existence of automobiles has changed our courtship patterns, our sexual practices, and especially our environment. It perfectly demonstrates the powerful impact of technology on our lives.

Twenty-five percent of our economy is tied up with the automotive business, if we count not just the manufacture of automobiles but the roads and services designed to accommodate them. We think we invented the automobile but, in fact, the automobile also invented us.

For example, the automobile has added burdens to parenthood which no other society in history has ever had to cope with. Surburban parents must now chauffeur their children everywhere. In the past, because there were so few automobiles, children could explore the community in relative safety. But the existence of automobiles has made leaving their own yards quite dangerous.

One could say, then, that the automobile has led to a whole new strategy of parenthood: fenced backyards and the notion that we must keep our children under surveillance at all times. This responsibility was never a part of parenthood when children could move about safely. The automobile has thus contributed to increased feelings of anxiety and frustration in parents. When these feelings are coupled with feelings of isolation (which, in some cases, can be traced to the suburbanization created by the automobile), they often lead to violence, helping to create a level of child abuse in our society that is one of the highest in the world. So, incredibly, we find the automobile influencing parenthood in a way no one would ever have dreamed.

The Design of Organizations

Technology always invents us. Organizations, for example, are shaped by the available communication technologies. Our earliest organizations, the tribes, had to conduct their business essentially within earshot. As it became possible to send messages over a distance, more diverse social organizations evolved. Mail and postal systems enabled centralized business organizations to come into being. The telephone and telegraph fostered the international organization.

The computer has created new, virtually officeless organizations. Business communications must now extend beyond the traditional geographic limits of the building that houses the organization to include employees in the field as well as clients, customers, consultants, and even competitors. McDonnell Douglas, in reinventing its communications system, had to include its principal competitor, Lockheed. To compete at one level, McDonnell Douglas had to collaborate at another.

Computer networking creates "communities" unlike any we have known before. Although the members may never be in the same room with each other, they develop strong working relationships and powerful bonds of friendship. This results partly from the fact that the technology invites people to "speak" more openly and candidly than they would in ordinary meetings. Relationships can become as intimate and deeply personal as any developed through face-to-face communication.

That phenomenon shouldn't surprise us. Throughout history, some of the most profound political discussions and the greatest love affairs have been conducted by people writing to each other. We tend to think that the best communication takes place where people can see and touch each other, but that is not necessarily so. Obviously, there are occasions where physical proximity is necessary. But face-to-face communication often introduces more "noise" in the system and imposes more limitations on personal expression. Paradoxically, the very technology that threatens to depersonalize our society offers a way to connect people, to restore a sense of community in our lives, to deepen our relationships.

At the same time, the advent of the computer and the advanced communications systems that it has made possible have raised difficult new questions: What is the appropriate span of control of a manager in a computerized network? What is to be the nature of that supervision? What is the role of middle management when vertical access from the top to the bottom of the organization (and vice versa) is made so easy? Will this technology democratize or centralize? What about issues of privacy, loyalty, identity, and secrecy?

A Life of Its Own

All these questions arise because technology has literally reinvented us. We are and will be different than we were. For the most part, we don't yet know in what ways those differences will express themselves, just as we did not anticipate the ways in which the automobile changed us.

We have always believed that technology is under our control—that it is neutral, benign—and that it is only our use of it that is suspect. But such is not the case. Technology develops a life of its own. It is autonomous. As Emerson noted, "Things are in the saddle and ride mankind." Imagine our trying to rid ourselves of the automobile, the television, or the computer. Impossible.

Technology rolls over us like an unstoppable juggernaut, and the possibilities of influencing it are quite limited. Moreover, the consequences of applying technology are likely to be different from our expectations, and very often the opposite of our intent. Only by understanding this can managers intelligently apply technology, assess its effects, and be reasonably prepared to cope with the unpredictable eventualities it will cause.

PART THREE

The Paradoxes of Communication

9

The More We Communicate, the Less We Communicate

THE NOTION THAT people need to communicate more is perhaps the most widely accepted idea in management, indeed in all human relationships. Whether it's called "counseling," "team building," "conflict resolution," or "negotiating," it all boils down to one idea—that if we talk it over, things will get better.

Well, yes and no. I certainly won't say that we don't need to talk. But communication, like everything else in human affairs, seldom works the way we think it does. Most organizations, in fact, are *overcommunicating*: meetings, conferences, memos, phone calls, and electronic mail overwhelm managers and employees alike. Increasingly, we seem to believe that everybody should be in on everything.

The classic experiment that put the lie to that belief was conducted many years ago by management consultant and organizational psychologist Alex Bavelas. This study, which came to be known as the "line and circle experiment," divided participants into two groups. In one, all information was fed by the group members to a central person—top-down line management, you might say. In the other, the information was shared around a circle, more like participative management.

Both groups were given the same problem to solve; for

example, each member of each group was given a box of different-colored marbles and the groups were then asked to identify the one color that was common to all boxes. When the marbles were all of solid colors, making them easier to distinguish and to describe, the line group did much better than the group in a circle. But then the problem was changed slightly to make it more complex; the marbles were no longer solid colors but were more mottled in design. The circle group, where each person could talk to the next person, not just the "leader," adjusted to the change more quickly and therefore did better than the line group.

These findings have been used to support the idea of participative management for many years. One of the lesser-known findings of the research, however, is of special interest to us. When all lines of communication were open—when participants could talk not only to the persons next to them but to all the other members of the group—then the problem-solving ability of the group diminished markedly and it became virtually paralyzed. In other words, there seems always to be an optimal level of communication beyond which further or expanded communication becomes dysfunctional. Communication has its limits.

A Formula for Tedium

Complete communication can be quite boring. In one management training exercise often done to demonstrate both the difficulty and the importance of achieving accurate communication, participants are not allowed to speak unless they first satisfy the previous speaker that his or her remarks were fully understood. This is done by repeating the previous speaker's message—not in a parroting way, but in one's own words—and then obtaining his or her agreement that the summation is accurate. Not surprisingly, this agreement is often hard to get. Eventually, participants learn the necessity and value of careful listening.

When the experiment is continued beyond a few minutes, however, it begins to wear on the participants. Even though the heat has gone out of the discussion and people are fully understanding each other, an enormous amount of boredom sets in. Accurate communication has become both tedious and stifling. The exercise reminds us that the transfer of accurate information is only a small part of the role communication plays in our lives.

Power Problems in Disguise

Many supposed communication problems are actually balance-of-power problems. That is why it probably is unwise to introduce completely open communication into a situation in which there is a large disparity in power. The unintended but damaging result is to increase the power of the already powerful and reduce the power of the already powerless. For example, in marriage counseling, if the person who feels rejected is asked to communicate his or her needs to the person doing the rejecting, it can actually worsen matters by making the rejected person even less attractive and more vulnerable to the other person.

The same is true in boss-employee relationships. When subordinates are asked to communicate honestly with their superiors, they run the risk of becoming more vulnerable, with potentially harmful consequences. One wonders how many people there are like one woman I know who was encouraged by her associates to go to her boss and "clear the air." She did and was fired soon afterward. It is only when the balance of power is relatively equal that truly candid communication can and should take place.

Enough Already

Organizations that believe all their troubles can be solved through increased communication may be in for a surprise. In a research project conducted by the Western Behavioral Sciences Institute, we set up an experimental information center at a major aerospace corporation. Employees who needed answers to questions could call the center to get them. To our initial puzzlement, the more the center succeeded in satisfying the questioners and the more popular it became, the more nervous management grew.

The company's executives were concerned that the chain of command was being circumvented ("If employees don't know something, they should ask their supervisors!"), that non-work-related questions were being asked ("Who can sing bass in a Christmas quartet?"), and that the organization might have difficulty accommodating such a potentially active service ("What if the center gets thousands of calls a day?"). When calls reached several hundred a day, the center was discontinued. The episode illustrated that rapid and accurate communication of information may be less important to management than are other organizational concerns.

Data Don't Matter

Most top-level executives make little use of the computers that connect them to their company's management information systems. The usual explanation is that they are computer naive. But it is more likely that the information systems are not giving executives what they want and need. Absurdly, we have management information systems that do not serve management.

These systems to gather and store mountains of data almost always ignore the actual needs of executives in favor of what others, operating on the basis of their best guesses, imagine these executives' needs to be. The guesses are based on what surely are logical assumptions—executives need personnel statistics, inventory display, sales figures, and the like. But almost all of this information is quantitative rather than qualitative and is of little use to top managers, who are dealing with predicaments that seldom yield to logical analysis.

What these executives require is more likely to come from the advice of their colleagues than from comprehensive displays of data. They need interpretations, opinions, information that has been "massaged." That is why executives spend almost all their time communicating—in meetings, in memos, or on the phone. Given the choice between data and each other, they choose each other.

Soon the computer will be ubiquitous, invisibly embedded everywhere in our work environments, sensitive to our working styles. It already carries text, voice, sound, both moving and still images, graphics, machine translation, an astounding array of databases, and more. Engineers are confident that this impressive technology will eventually make its way into the executive suite. But to genuinely serve top management, information systems must be based on studies of the real interactions of top executives. Designed from the top down, as it were, an information system might then emerge that actually serves the strategic interests of organizations. But until then, no chance.

10

In Communication, Form Is More Important Than Content

WHEN WE WITNESS a red-faced executive shouting, "Who's excited? I'm not excited!" we realize that the feeling is much more important than the words. That's why in all communication it's crucial to listen to the music as well as the lyrics, the feeling behind the words as well as the words themselves.

Similarly, we are well aware that a written message carries more weight than a spoken one, and among written messages one that is printed is weightier than one that is typed, which is weightier than one that is handwritten, even though the words may be identical. The mode of expression, it would seem, is more important than the words.

We all realize, for example, that when a telephone call to a company is answered by a receptionist with a British accent, that person is likely to convey an image of being unusually intelligent and better organized, creating a positive impression of the corporation itself. Indeed, the idea of corporate image conveyed in letterheads, annual reports, advertising, and even buildings is a triumph of form over content.

The Power of the Invisible

One of the most subtle examples of this phenomenon is something I call *metamessages*. They tend to be invisible but are nevertheless indelible. Consider, for instance, the hidden curriculum of a school as described by social critic Ivan Illich. We all are aware that adults do not retain much of what they were taught in school as children. Most of us could not pass a seventh-grade history exam or calculate a square root, even though we once could.

But we all retain what was taught in the hidden curriculum. We learned to sit still, raise our hands, wait in line, obey adult authority, and ask permission. We also learned that teachers tend to be women and administrators men, that there are things we can talk about and things we shouldn't, and so forth. We never forgot these lessons, because they were taught not as part of the actual curriculum but rather by the ritual or form of education. Each was a metamessage.

In all of life, the metamessage tends to be more powerful than the message itself. I see this in management training programs, in particular. The very existence of such programs conveys the mistaken message—even for those people who do not take the training—that management is a skill that can be taught and learned quickly. But as I have noted earlier, effective management is not a matter of acquiring skills. There are many ways to do the job. When the metamessages of management training programs say otherwise, an impossible burden is imposed on even seasoned managers. Invariably, their newly acquired "skills" desert them. They end up feeling inadequate and obliged to take action, any action, with sometimes regrettable consequences.

Where We Sit Matters

For another example of form over content, look at how we arrange ourselves at business meetings. There is a great difference between sitting at the customary oblong table, with the leader at the head, and sitting around a circular table at which no distinction is made for the leader. The same people with the same agenda may be seated at both tables, but a very different meeting ensues.

If the table is removed and people are seated in a circle of chairs, exposed to each other, the meeting will also be predictably different. It will become even more different if people remove their jackets and ties, and still more different if they take off their shoes and sit on the floor. At each of these stages, the discussion becomes less formal, more participative, more personal. Nothing has changed except the form, and yet because of that, everything has changed.

We are only too well aware of the metamessages in the design of an office. Almost anyone will become more intimidating when they sit in a large corner office with carpeting, an expansive desk, a leather chair with a high back, and other symbols of executive authority.

Remembering the Rituals

All of this teaches us that we may be so concerned about the content of what we say or write that we often forget the form. Yet the feelings, the rituals, the arrangements, the social and physical design—all that is implied by the way we organize and communicate an experience—are crucially important. When they are taken into account, it is possible to send metamessages that are consonant with the intended message and reinforce rather than undermine it.

11

Listening Is More Difficult Than Talking

WHEN WE GENUINELY listen to another person, we are able to enter a special world in which feelings are shared. That's a rare experience, rewarding for both parties. It yields so many positive consequences that teaching listening skills has become standard in the repertoire of management trainers. But if listening is so satisfying and effective, why don't we find more of it in the workplace? Why don't managers listen more?

For many reasons. One important reason is that good listening is inordinately difficult, even for experienced listeners. It is unrealistic to expect people to learn it quickly or to do it easily. One need only to go through the back and forth of trying to get another person to agree, "Yes, that's what I really mean," to discover how difficult it is. We fail far more often than we succeed.

In some situations, listening may even be inappropriate. Leaders at times need to ignore others, follow their own lights, tenaciously hold to a course of action. Genuine listening to others' views need not derail such action, but it could. Presidents Jimmy Carter and Bill Clinton, both excellent listeners, have both been faulted for spending too much time listening, trying to build consensus.

In listening, managers may feel confined, having to focus

entirely upon what the other person means, how he or she sees the world. Ordinarily, human beings need more psychological space in which to move in their communication. Listening denies the listener that space.

It's something like driving a car. We don't focus on the road all the time. That would be too confining. We look at the scenery, eat, drink, talk, sing, hug, kiss, play the radio. People fail to listen not just because they don't know how, but because they feel capable of so much more than the demands of listening permit.

The Obstacles Encountered

Listening can also be a disturbing experience. All of us have strong needs to see the world in certain ways, and when we really listen, so that we understand the other person's perspective, we risk being changed ourselves. Similarly, listening to others means having to be alert to one's own defensiveness, to one's impulse to want to change others. That requires a level of self-awareness, even self-criticism, that is often not easy to endure.

Listening demands openness, trust, and respect, qualities difficult to maintain and seldom exhibited in any uniform way even by the most experienced listeners. It is more an attitude than a skill. The best kind of listening comes not from technique but from being genuinely interested in what really matters to the other person. Listening is much more than patiently hearing people out.

For managers, listening poses a special dilemma. Research tells us that people are more likely to change when we reverse the flow of communication, that is, when people are not talked at but when they themselves have a chance to talk. Yet the popular view persists that our leaders must be great communicators, inspiring and succeeding because of their speaking ability, *not* their listening ability. It can be difficult for managers to reconcile those competing requirements.

Finally, it has been thought that listening would be contagious, that those who were listened to sensitively would gain the ability to listen to others in the same way. Unfortunately, that's probably not what actually happens. The listening model does not seem to spread in the way one might hope, or if it does, it is in small measure.

Not the Stuff of Manipulation

A booklet Carl Rogers and I wrote in 1955 introduced the phrase "active listening" into the lexicon of management and human relations training. Even though I pretty much agree with what we said then, I would not write such a piece today. The main reason is that I no longer believe that genuine listening should be reduced to a technique.

To me, there is something graceless and manipulative in analyzing those special moments when we are enriched and exhilarated by someone's listening to us, or being honest with us, or praising us, and teaching them as human relations or management skills. It is like learning memory tricks so that you can call someone you barely know by name, or using self-disclosure as a method of gaining someone's confidence. Unfortunately, the entire range of human emotional response has become fair game for the management technologists.

12

Praising People Does Not Motivate Them

I HAVE LONG questioned the cherished idea that people work better after being praised. I realize that here I am in unfriendly territory, because praise is perhaps the most widely used and thoroughly endorsed of all human relations techniques. Parents, managers, psychologists, teachers—everyone seems to believe in its value as a motivational tool, a reward, a way to establish good relationships. We value it because we have all experienced the thrill of discovering that someone we respect thinks highly of us.

But I doubt that praise, when consciously employed as a management technique, always accomplishes what we think it does. Not that it does not have valuable functions (of which we are largely unaware), but I think our beliefs about its *motivational* value need closer scrutiny. Consider the following.

Praise may, in fact, be perceived as threatening. Watch how people respond to praise. Don't they often react with discomfort or uneasiness? A very common response is a vague denial or derogation: "I really can't take the credit for it," or "You're just saying that." Praise a house or garden and its owner may hasten to point out its defects; praise an employee for a project and that person is sometimes quick to play down his or her role in it. The defensiveness is compounded, of course, when the praise is unearned or undeserved.

People react defensively because in praise there can be threat. After all, praise *is* an evaluation, and to be evaluated, to be judged, usually makes us uncomfortable—even if the evaluation is positive. Additionally, when you praise people, you are often trying to motivate them, to move them in certain directions, to *change* them. The threat of change is nearly always disquieting.

Instead of reassuring people about their worth, praise may be a way of gaining status over them. Giving praise establishes the fact that you are in a position to sit in judgment. A manager evaluating an employee needs to be sensitive to this. Even if the evaluation is positive, the employee can end up feeling diminished if it seems the manager is merely reinforcing his or her status.

Interestingly, when the work of a high-status person is praised by a low-status person, it is often seen as presumptuous or even insulting. If an ordinary person were to have told Picasso, "You're a very good painter," that compliment would not likely have been particularly well received. In order to be acceptable, the praise must be given in a way that respects the status difference: "I love your painting."

Praise may constrict creativity rather than free it. Some actions by managers are intended as rewards—like salaries and benefits. But because the employee has come to take them for granted, they no longer function as rewards. That can also be true with praise. When we demand it, and it is routinely given, it no longer serves to motivate us.

What really does release creativity and promote achievement is when a manager takes the time to get *involved* in the employee's work—learning what direction the work is taking, the problems and possibilities it presents, the way the employee is dealing with the task. But involvement is demanding and time-consuming, which probably explains why many managers resort to praise as a substitute, hoping that it will accomplish the same results.

Praise can come to be associated mainly with criticism. This happens when we use praise to sugarcoat blame, or employ the "sandwich technique," whereby praise is followed by reproof, then repeated. "I'm very pleased with your work, Fred," says the boss. "You're really getting the work out, *but...*" Fred then hears the unhappy part of the story, the reprimand. The boss finishes up with "Keep up the fine work," and Fred is shuttled out without quite knowing what hit him.

This is also a favorite technique of parents and teachers. And we have become so conditioned by its use from early childhood that when we are praised, we automatically get ready for the shock, the reproof.

Rather than functioning as a bridge between people, praise may actually put distance between them. In a society that fills our daily lives with so many contacts, we need to find ways to establish distance—psychological elbow room—between ourselves and others. Praise is one of the most effective simply because, when we evaluate people, we are not likely to gain emotional proximity to them. See for yourself if praise doesn't tend to hold off, to separate, while other behaviors—like listening—tend to include, to embrace.

Rather than opening the way to further contact, praise may be a means of terminating it. Think how often we use praise as a sign that a conversation or interview is over. "It's good to talk with you" means "I've finished talking with you." And "You're doing fine; keep up the good work" usually signals the end of a conversation.

When Praise Matters

Praise also helps to keep patterns of relationships between people in organizations relatively stable, allowing hierarchies or structures to be maintained. How does praise work toward this end? Let's take as an example a problem-solving committee meeting that includes the executive vice president at one end of the hierarchy and a new junior assistant at the other. If the assistant comes up with the brightest and most useful idea, some way must be found to accept it without lowering the status of the vice president in the eyes of the group, thereby threatening the group's stability. Intuitively, the vice president may say to the young assistant, "That's a very good idea. We can use that."

This not-so-simple act of praise has resolved the situation nicely. Status has been maintained (because, as we remember, praise is a way of claiming status); the young assistant has been reminded of his place in the hierarchy; and the group is restored to comfortable equilibrium. In this situation and others like it, praise is a lubricant that helps keep our human relations in good working order.

The fundamental issue with praise has to do with its credibility, which has eroded because it is used for so many purposes other than simply expressing appreciation. But on those all-too-infrequent occasions when it is believable—for example, when we read a letter written to a third party in which the writer speaks highly of us, not knowing that we will ever see the letter—praise is welcome indeed.

PART FOUR

The Politics of Management

13

Every Act Is a Political Act

I'VE ALWAYS THOUGHT of myself as being in the business of human liberation. Yet over the years, while working as a psychologist, a therapist, or a consultant, I have tried to "cure" homosexuals, to teach bosses to "manage" employees, to train teachers to "handle" students, and to help parents "control" children. In each case I was working for the powerful against the powerless, and doing it in the name of a professional attempt at human liberation.

My experience has made me rethink my conduct as a manager. I have come to realize that every management act is a political act. By this I mean that every management act in some way redistributes or reinforces power. As managers, we sometimes engage in these acts consciously, as when we take care to promote African-Americans and other minorities over their white counterparts. But most often we perform these acts unconsciously, as when we direct our conversation more to the men in a meeting than to the women.

Here are some other examples of political acts we might witness in an organization: Hiring a woman as a secretary and a man as a management trainee. Switching to part-time or contract employees to avoid paying benefits. Maintaining wage differentials between men and women. Hiring a relative. Building a ramp for handicapped workers. Staking out a corner office. Running an advertisement showing a woman admiring her clean laundry. Retiring people at age sixty-five, or very often younger.

When a woman friend of mine had a baby, she decided to give up her vice presidency and start an entrepreneurial enterprise that would enable her to work almost entirely from home. She wanted to be with her child during the early years. This was a political act, as are the actions being taken by many companies now—job sharing, flextime, tele-commuting, child care services—to keep such women from leaving.

For Your Own Good

Our inability as managers to think in political terms tends to make us look at people as if they have personal problems, when many times their problems are a result of their place in the power structure of our society. Modern life burdens people in so many ways that are independent of any personal qualities. They are buffeted about in crowded urban settings, or lonely and isolated in suburbs, or are weighed down by the effects of round-the-clock parenthood. Changes in their situations are much more likely to improve their lot in life than counseling them as if their problems were matters of personality or character. Similarly, making changes in the work environment—redesigning the office layout, shifting reporting relationships, altering schedules—is more likely to lead to behavior change than is, say, management training.

A highly regarded executive secretary I know began to make a lot of mistakes in her work. She was coached and counseled to no avail. Finally, because another executive was in a jam and without help, she was transferred to work with him. To everyone's relief, her work regained and even sur-passed its original excellent quality. A new environment and new relationships were all that it took.

Who are the managers who keep people from working at their best as a result of political discrimination? All of us, and we do it unknowingly. Very often these acts are committed with the best of intentions. There is a history, for example, of legislation by male lawmakers to protect women in the workplace—preventing them from having to lift heavy packages, guaranteeing them coffee breaks, providing cots in their rest rooms, and making it illegal to require overtime work.

But that very legislation has "protected" women into second-class status, many of them into poverty. Even now, women make only 75 percent of the pay men get for the same work. They are systematically excluded from management roles, because it has been difficult for many managers to see how someone who has to have a cot in her rest room or cannot be worked overtime should be put in a leadership position.

That is why we have civil rights—not only to protect us from bad people, but to protect us from good people as well, from people who think they know what's good for us. After all, tyrants have always acted in the best interests of their people, or so they thought.

The Important Feature

Having had my political consciousness raised a bit on these issues, I can now recognize that when I sit across the desk from a woman, the overwhelming feature of her life is that she *is* a woman. That one fact is likely to be more important to what she is experiencing in life than her personality, her character, or her behavior. The same is true for men.

At a men's group discussion I once attended, one member said that he would like to talk about what it's like to be in a men's rest room (where the urinals are against the wall, and when it is crowded men stand in lines facing each urinal, waiting their turn). Sometimes when a man gets to the head of the line and feels the pressure of those waiting behind him, he has difficulty starting his urinary flow. Within seconds, he begins to panic, sometimes zipping up and leaving rather than face the humiliation of standing there so long that those behind him begin to wonder.

Why, asked this man, are we supposed to be so good at this? And, of course, the answer was that it is part of the larger pressure on men to produce and perform. The members of the group were discovering the power of the sex role in areas of their lives they had never before considered.

A Useful Exercise

Managers understandably resist having to think in political terms, but the alternative is to run headlong into trouble that we won't see coming. Sometimes the outcome of this is costly, as it is when employees file suits for sexual harassment. But political consequences extend far beyond sexual politics.

I once involved a group of managers in an exercise to better understand the challenge they faced. Across the top of a blackboard, we listed various groups represented by liberation movements at the time (African-Americans, Latinos, Asians, women, men, children, gays, handicapped, and so on). Down the side, we listed areas of management decision-making (recruiting, staffing, training, compensation, production, marketing, advertising, facilities, communication, and so on). We then drew lines down and across the blackboard, creating a matrix in which each square represented the interaction of a management area with a liberation group.

We were soon into a lively discussion of the problems created or the advantages given to these groups in each management area. For example, at the juncture of facilities and women, the participants thought of the design of office space that creates what has been referred to pejoratively as a "henhouse"—a cluster of female secretaries and assistants in a windowless area surrounded by private offices for executives. They discussed recruiting that fails to solicit applications from overlooked groups such as the handicapped, choosing a plant site that would create transportation hardships for inner-city groups, automating production and thereby reducing the power of labor organizations, failing to promote overweight employees, and so on. The list of situations that this exercise generates is virtually endless, making it quite illuminating and consciousness-raising.

Such thinking will never become easy for us because it is impossible to predict the next group that will make liberation demands. But we can keep our minds open and responsive, remembering not to dismiss these new demands simply because we did not expect *that* group to be discontented. Initially, all such demands have appeared to most people to be wrong, puzzling, unfair, impertinent, even ridiculous. We have learned that, in time, this perception changes.

A Balancing Act

It would be naive to suggest that greater political awareness will occur without setbacks. In fact, lately we have worked ourselves into a troubling predicament. Fighting for the rights of special groups has contributed to an erosion of civility that none of us anticipated. When people are treated as representatives of special groups, society is fragmented. It may even be that progress on rights has been made at the expense of the common welfare. Enmity grows between groups as they compete for rights. Rather than looking after the community, each group looks after itself. The common welfare suffers. The achievement and preservation of community must become our top priority. Otherwise, the concept of rights has no meaning. Rights to what, if not access to community?

Sometimes the realization that every act is a political act can seem paralyzingly absurd, and the demands of group politics further complicate the already complex realities that managers face every day. Nevertheless, we cannot turn away from them. Rather, we must balance our accommodations to them with an exercise of judgment that assures the stability and success of the total organization.

14

The Best Resource for the Solution of Any Problem Is the Person or Group That Presents the Problem

EX-CONVICTS ARE BETTER able to rehabilitate prison inmates than is the prison staff. Ex–drug addicts are more successful in getting other addicts off drugs than are psychiatrists. Students learn more from each other than they do from their professors. People tend to be much smarter about their own situations than we give them credit for. After all, a full grasp of any problem is only in the hands of the people who have experienced it.

In the early 1940s when Carl Rogers claimed that people with problems might be in the best position to know what to do about them, the professional world responded with disbelief and ridicule. How could the very people who were suffering from a problem know how to solve it? This idea was heresy to professionals trained to think that problems could be solved only by bringing to bear their own analytic ability and therapeutic skills.

But this idea has since gained acceptance in practically every professional area, including management. It is not practiced uniformly of course, because sometimes experts can help, and people are not always the best judges of their own situations. Nevertheless, Rogers's belief, which at one time seemed absurd, now has wide currency.

Community planners, for example, recognize the efficacy of involving the people for whom the plans are being made in each stage of the process. It leads not only to wider acceptance of a plan but improves it, because these people often have a keen awareness of issues that professionals have not fully assessed.

The clearest validation of this approach is the proliferation of self-help groups. Alcoholics Anonymous, the most famous of these groups that meet without professional leadership, clearly has a better record of keeping people away from alcohol than the professions dedicated to that effort. There are now thousands of self-help organizations reaching many millions of people, ranging from Weight Watchers to Parents Without Partners to Gamblers Anonymous. Each of them demonstrates the power of people who are themselves beset with the problems and yet are able to help each other in ways that the professionals have not yet learned to do.

We can rely on people in this way because within all of us lies a mastery of roles that we rarely if ever play, each requiring complex skills we have somehow learned through the natural course of our lives. That is the basic reason why managers can become effective even though they may never have had a day of formal training. They already know how.

Widely Approved, Seldom Practiced

Participative management—involving the people who have to do the work in the decisions that will affect them—is based upon the idea that people are better than we think they are and can be counted on to make wise choices. A considerable amount of research shows that people learn faster, produce more, and are more highly motivated when participative methods are employed. The challenge for management is how to tap this powerful resource. No one knows the ceiling of performance when the proper expectations are introduced and the appropriate social architecture is in place.

But here is another paradox: While the participative approach is widely agreed to be effective, it is seldom put into practice. Companies experiment with it, but few employ participative management in a continuing organization-wide manner. Why is that so? One answer, of course, is that managers do not like to demean their own expertise by assuming that the group can do it better. But there are other reasons, too.

Participative management depends on trusting the group. Most managers simply don't have that confidence and can't take the time to develop that trust. Even when groups are consulted, they don't always believe in themselves and so may resist the idea of involvement. And let's face it, it can take an inordinate amount of time and patience to develop a group that can practice participative management. One must have the patience of a saint to sit through meetings where the group may spend thirty minutes talking about the coffee machine.

Companies also stumble by pursuing participative management ideas that are overly simplistic and do not acknowledge the complexities of organizational behavior. Many companies fail to recognize that the participative approach requires a somewhat different leader who is tuned in to the undercurrents and the hidden agendas that accompany any meeting.

Finally, managers who experiment with participative methods open themselves up to abuse. Groups that are testing their leaders' ability to hear what they are saying or to accept their ideas can humiliate the leaders by resisting attempts to evoke participation. In such situations, managers who try to elicit ideas often become the focus of the group's complaints. Sometimes there even is open hostility.

Mary Douglas, the noted British anthropologist, once explained to me that participative systems are importantly different from hierarchical systems not just in the way that risks are assesssed and decisions made, but also in the ways people are treated. The introduction of highly participative systems tends to bring attacks on the stronger members, often the leaders, while more hierarchical systems bring attacks on the weaker members.

I remember consulting at a university in which the provost of one of the colleges was committed to a participative approach. All matters that needed deciding were brought before the students and faculty. The entering freshmen were impressed that they could express themselves so freely, that they could challenge the provost, even use obscenities with him and get away with it. It was so exhilarating to the young people that they neglected to appreciate the debilitating effect on the provost. Each incoming class would go through somewhat the same ritual, testing and abusing the leader. Over a period of a couple of years, I witnessed the gradual wearing down of the provost, who had undertaken the experiment with unbridled energy and enthusiasm. He resigned his post in the third year, and the program reverted to a traditional form.

Conserving the Human Resources

That experience was one of many that led me to take what I would call a *conservation of resources* approach to consulting with groups. I now tend to begin my consultation by asking the group to identify its most valuable resources—typically, human resources, usually the group leader and the most creative individuals in the group. Then I explore with the group the ways these resources could be protected, enhanced, and conserved.

More often than not, the group will realize on its own that these individuals require expressions of appreciation, recognition, even some deference. The group itself will often come up with ways to respect the special needs of these individuals—for example, understanding that at times they need to be able to close their doors or to work unusual hours. Instead of complaining about the leadership styles, work habits, or idiosyncrasies of its colleagues, the group designs ways to accommodate them. The process provides a foundation on which to build discussions of more fundamental issues.

PART FIVE

Organizational Predicaments

15

Organizations That Need Help Most Will Benefit from It Least

DEEPLY TROUBLED COMPANIES don't usually seek help. And when they do, they have a hard time benefiting from it. The situation parallels one in psychotherapy. Psychotherapy is usually ineffective for severely mentally ill people; it works better for well people. The healthier you are psychologically, or the less you may seem to need to change, the more you can change.

It is no accident that most psychotherapists do not work in mental hospitals but instead have office practices where they deal with people who are functioning relatively well. Psychotherapists have much more to offer such people. In the same way, management consultants most often work with relatively healthy organizations. They are seldom called into the most troubled organizations and, in fact, have little to offer them.

The consultant's essential role is to hold up a mirror to the organization, reflecting the processes that may be limiting its growth. As might be expected, the most critical issues center around leadership, not performance down the line. Small wonder, then, that leaders of troubled companies tend to shy away from calling in consultants. They know that they will have to do some serious self-examination.

Looking for the Easy Fix

Most often what gets organizations into trouble are faulty leadership styles, poor internal relationships, and managerial blind spots. The delusional hope of a troubled organization is that it will be saved without having to make changes in these highly personal areas. Perhaps the market will turn around, a loan will come through, there will be a new technique to apply to handle a difficult employee, competitors will give up, or the new product will succeed.

The hope is that no members of the organization will have to make wrenching changes in the way they work together, or in their personal beliefs about themselves and the ways they make decisions. Thus, even when experts are called into troubled companies, the managers most often seek impersonal solutions—better ways to select new executives, a new formula for success, a new series of pep talks. They are seldom prepared for the intensive self-examination that is so often necessary to reach the core of the problem.

Calamity versus Good Times

What about the belief that a crisis will bring organizations around to the recognition that help is needed—that when the trouble has reached calamitous proportions, people are forced to look at themselves? Not necessarily so.

While it is true that a crisis often forces change, and (as we will see in a later chapter) calamity can be very helpful to an organization, neither makes it more likely that the organization will undergo a real self-examination. Resistance is simply too strong, too deep. What is more likely is that massive layoffs will occur; stockholders will force leadership changes; radical and sometimes long overdue reorganization will be undertaken. But the ways in which a management consultant can be helpful are not likely to command much attention at that stage of events.

At the other end of the success spectrum, when profits are plentiful because the company has hit upon an enormously successful product or captured an inordinately large share of the market, almost any managerial practice is acceptable. Affluence may foster magnanimous treatment of employees, but it is not always the best climate for self-evaluation.

So by a "healthy organization," I don't necessarily mean an affluent one. In an affluent organization one can get away with almost anything. Indeed, it is common for the leaders of such organizations to attribute their success to managerial practices that might not be at all effective in a less favorable business climate.

Who Changes, Who Doesn't

Although company leaders sometimes call in consultants to help make other people change, the paradox is that the people they want most to change will change least. Instead, that responsibility usually devolves to the leaders themselves, because they are more capable of making change.

This can be a frustrating experience for the leader. I once consulted with an organization whose president was impatient with the behavior of one of his senior staff members and wanted me to straighten this man out. As it happened, this difficult staff member was also the most creative and hardworking person in the organization, responsible for the most important area of the company's work. But he was indeed intransigent.

Because of his extraordinary value to the organization, and because of the seeming hopelessness of his ever changing, I worked instead with the president to help him adapt his own behavior to accommodate this person. While that may seem unfair, the president was the only one who could make the necessary changes and keep the organization productive.

Typically, people want someone else to change, and often for good reason. But for the consultant, the general rule is that the person who *can* change is the one to work with, and usually that is the person who has brought the situation to the consultant in the first place. The absurd, but entirely practical, approach is that we ask the people who need to change least to do the changing.

16

Individuals Are Almost Indestructible, but Organizations Are Very Fragile

I HAVE BEEN impressed again and again by how resilient individuals are, but how fragile are the organizations that are key to their survival.

Even the most intense, confrontational, and sometimes traumatic situations rarely damage an individual. Yes, there is hurt, but seldom is there permanent damage. People survive the most devastating natural disasters in relatively good psychological shape. But relationships can be destroyed with one wrong word, one single act. That has important implications for organizations, particularly small ones. Most businesses fail because of ruptured relationships among the principals.

Commonly held ideas about the fragility of individuals have led us to treat people who have gone through horrifying experiences such as the Holocaust as if they were damaged goods. So we compound their hurt by regarding them as somehow less than fully capable. That is not to say people don't suffer, but they are not damaged to a point where they function less than normally. A former student of mine, Edith Egers, a survivor of Auschwitz, discovered this when she conducted a study of other Holocaust survivors. While they were no doubt deeply scarred, on all life-adjustment and personality measures they functioned as well as or better than others who had not experienced such traumatic ordeals.

Fragile Monoliths

Individuals are very strong, but organizations are not. Part of the reason why we don't recognize the vulnerability of organizations is that we have a hard time believing that the relationships which make them work are real. Even psychologists sometimes think of organizations as simply collections of individuals. But relationships—the bonds between people —are very real, and they have a life of their own. To a great extent they determine the behavior of an organization and the people within it.

We may also feel that we can abuse organizations because we have all had experiences with bureaucracies that make them seem like monoliths, impenetrable to all our efforts to make them respond. We feel we have no impact on organizations, that no matter what we do, they can absorb it. That, of course, is not the case. One bad press story can severely damage a bureaucracy. Even giant corporations that seem indestructible can be seriously wounded or even brought down by a single unfortunate turn of events, as we have recently seen with the bankruptcy of Dow-Corning as a result of lawsuits filed on behalf of the recipients of the company's silicone breast implants, and with the closure of Johns-Manville because of litigation over the health hazards of asbestos.

Not all companies deserve to survive but, nevertheless, we should be paying more attention as a society to sustaining organizations. We cannot assume that because they are large they are also invincible. A troubled or failing organization needs at least as much attention as a troubled or failing individual. After all, our lives depend upon organizations. For all practical purposes, in terms of our ability to understand and improve the way society functions, it may be that the individual is the wrong focus of our attention. Perhaps we should be looking more carefully at constellations of individuals, groups, families, work teams.

My experience tells me that people suffer most in their lives from failed or failing relationships—parental rejections, marital strife, difficulties with bosses—or from the lack of relationships—isolation, alienation, erosion of community. It follows, then, that the best way to deal with individuals may be to improve relationships.

17

The Better Things Are, the Worse They Feel

WHEN WE MANAGERS take action to improve situations, we expect that our efforts will produce satisfaction for those we try to help. But they seldom do—not for long anyway. The paradox is that improvement in human affairs leads not to satisfaction but to discontent, albeit a higher-order discontent than might have existed before.

The history of revolutions is an example. Revolutions start not when conditions are at their worst, but only after they have begun to improve, reforms have been instituted, leadership has developed, and the populace has come to have a new vision of what might be. The people may have been miserable before, but they did not exhibit the particular kind of discontent that comes from expecting things to be better. This is what historians have labeled the *theory of rising expectations.* It fuels the fires of revolution and change because it creates a discrepancy between what people have and what they now see is possible to have. That discrepancy is the source of discontent and the engine for change.

Psychotherapy works the same way. Successful therapy leads not to satisfaction but to new and different feelings of discontent. That is, as people solve the lower-order problems that brought them to therapy, instead of becoming contented, they become discontented about higher-order issues.

This was demonstrated in a research project conducted by a former student of mine, psychologist Marcine Johnson. In her study, patients began their psychotherapy by describing themselves in low-level terms: "I feel fatigued most of the time." "I worry about job security." Then, as therapy progressed, they began to express midlevel concerns: "I don't get enough appreciation from others." "I need to find some friends with whom to share things." By the end of therapy, they had developed high-order discontent: "I need to take more pride in who I am." "I wish I could accomplish something more significant."

Why is this phenomenon important to understand? Because the motivation for continuing change and growth comes from the development of higher-quality discontent, then moving on to the solution of more important problems.

Listening to the Grumbles

Psychologist Abraham Maslow had an interesting way of describing this phenomenon as it applied to the health of organizations. He advised managers to listen not for the presence or absence of complaints, but rather to what people were complaining about—that is, the quality or level of the complaint. He called them "grumbles." In the least healthy organizations, Maslow said, you can expect to hear low-order grumbles—complaints about working conditions, about what he called "deficiency needs." For example: "It's too hot in here." Or, "I don't get paid enough."

In a healthier organization, Maslow said, there would be high-order grumbles—complaints that extend beyond the self to more altruistic concerns: "Did you hear what happened to the people over in Plant Two? They really got cheated." Or, "We need better safety standards around here." But in a *very* healthy organization, there would be "metagrumbles"—complaints having to do with needs for self-actualization: "I don't feel that my talents are being fully utilized." Or, "I don't feel that I'm in on things enough around here."

There is the absurdity. Only in an organization where people *are* in on things and where their talents *are* being utilized would it occur to someone to complain about those issues. What this means to the manager is that improvement does not bring contentment but its opposite. Absurd as it seems, the way to judge your effectiveness is to assess the quality of the discontent you engender, the ability to produce movement from low-order discontent to high-order discontent.

This is useful to keep in mind no matter how innocuous the issue might seem. The relaxation of dress codes in many corporations has made it possible on one or more days a week for employees to forgo coats and ties, or dresses and heels. Managers who expected their staffs to be pleased by such policy changes must instead be nonplussed by the welter of demands, questions, and complaints that have resulted.

It isn't just that the new policy confuses people. They are simply doing what people normally do whose situations have been improved. Easing the dress codes raises expectations for further change, and they now want more informal days, looser codes, clearer policies. Pity the poor manager who can't imagine how a well-intended action led to such grousing.

A Dumbfounding Dynamic

The paradox of rising expectations helps us better understand why it is on the best campuses that there is the most restlessness and demand for change; in the cities where there are the greatest strides in race relations that we have higher tensions; and in countries making their way toward democratic change that there are the most troublesome demands from the population.

The liberalizing events in eastern Europe and China can be interpreted this way. Most observers of the European upheaval believed the demands for more freedom were the result of repression and long-festering frustrations. But if we were to follow that highly logical and commonsense line of reasoning, then those who had suffered the most repression and had had the most hard-line leaders would be the ones who protested most strongly. That did not seem to be what happened. Those European countries with the harshest and most repressive hard-line leadership were the last to leave the communist orbit. The protests were not as loud in Romania or Bulgaria as they were in countries such as East Germany, Poland, Hungary, and Czechoslovakia, where the hard line had been abandoned for some time. And in the Soviet Union, ironically, it was the great reformer Gorbachev, the architect of glasnost and perestroika, who was the one to be forced out.

It is surely no coincidence that in China the Tiananmen Square protests erupted after the country's leaders had done more to open China to the world than perhaps any other rulers in the nation's history. Those leaders must have been dumbfounded when they were made targets of the protests. They had doubled the wealth of China in a decade, and had instituted all manner of quasi-democratic and capitalistic reforms. And what did they get for it? From their perspective, angry, protesting, thankless students. But instead of evaluating their success on the quality of discontent they had created, they became angry themselves and resorted to the massive repression for which their backgrounds had well prepared them. The students, like their counterparts in eastern Europe, were calling for the removal of the very leaders who had instituted the reforms on which their new expectations were based.

In Marriage, Different Complaints

This paradox of rising expectations also supports the argument that good marriages—that is, those marriages that reflect what most people would want in marriage (love and affection, common interests, a good sex life, strong commitment to their children, etc.)— are more likely to fail than bad ones. Listen to the complaints of those recently divorced. You will seldom hear of brutality and desertion, but usually something like this: "We just don't communicate very well." "The educational differences between us were simply too great to overcome." "I felt trapped in the relationship."

People enter marriage with higher expectations than ever before. Couples now expect—even demand—communication and understanding, shared values and goals, intellectual companionship, full sexual lives, deep romantic love, great moments of intimacy—qualities that were not a part of the expectations in years past. When these escalating expectations are not met, even in marriages that seem ideal in most respects, high-order discontent results. Sometimes marriage actually delivers such peak moments, yet couples go on to burden the relationship with even greater demands.

Add to that the American idea that we must take action whenever we feel that we have a "problem." Too often, the only action that we can take is what I would call *terminal action*. We are unable to "fix" our marriages, so we end them, in the belief that we are taking responsible action. People treat jobs the same way. High-order discontent and the felt need for action lead many to quit their jobs. Quite unnecessarily, I suspect. All this may help to explain the absurdity that second marriages are better than first marriages, but shorter!

PART SIX

Dilemmas of Change

18

We Think We Want Creativity or Change, but We Really Don't

IN MY EXPERIENCE as a psychotherapist I continually wrestle with a fundamental paradox: Clients come to therapy seemingly wanting to change but then spend most of their time resisting it. This can be traced at least partly to their unwillingness to give up the pictures they have of themselves, pictures that have been developed over a lifetime. These self-images or self-concepts are all they have to identify themselves. Understandably, to abandon them could be deeply threatening.

I see the same resistance to change in management training programs, when people or groups are put into situations where there is freedom to operate differently than usual. Managers take part in these sessions presumably because they want to experience something new in their own personal relations. But they then join with the rest of the participants resisting that new experience by trying to create situations identical to the very ones that they dislike in their everyday lives. They seem compelled to make over the sessions into the most conventional kind of gatherings, with agendas, objectives, designated leadership, and so forth. It often takes quite a long time for groups to feel safe enough to explore different ways of operating.

Stifling Creativity

Although most people think otherwise, creative ideas are relatively easy to elicit. Usually, all you have to do is make the request—in brainstorming sessions, for example. But the good ideas that come from such creative encounters are only a small part of what it takes to institute change. To *implement* an idea is the tougher task.

I once ran an organization where we did our best to encourage innovation. But I sometimes felt that if one more person brought me another good idea I would lose whatever composure I still had, because I didn't know how I could manage what already was in front of me. The fundamental problem with creativity is that every really new idea requires the manager and the work force to undergo significant change. So it is no wonder that most organizations—schools, businesses, churches, and so on—seem to be designed for the express purpose of discouraging creativity.

We also stifle creativity because it usually means tapping the unconscious, the world of feelings. We fear emotionality, intimacy, vulnerability. Feelings are our enemies, we often think. We worry that if we unleash our deeper feelings we will be playing with fire. And so we censor ourselves and each other in all sorts of ways.

We play intellectual games. "Define that term." Or, "On what authority do you make that claim?"

We judge and evaluate. "You're using too much paint." Or, "It was better last time." (Both managers and employees so dread evaluation that performance reviews have come to have nothing to do with actual performance.)

We deal in absolutes. "We've always done it that way." Or, "We don't make exceptions around here."

We think in stereotypical ways. "I couldn't possibly work for a female boss." Or, "Men are rational, women are intuitive." All of these stereotypes condition our reactions and make it difficult for us to see the possibilities for change.

We don't trust our own experience, and we train our employees not to trust theirs. We tell them, "You're not ready to take on that responsibility," and gradually they do come to disregard their own experience and defer to the judgment of others.

Make It Manageable, Please

Real creativity, the kind that is responsible for breakthrough changes in our society, always violates the rules. That is why it is so unmanageable and that is why, in most organizations, when we say we desire creativity we really mean *manageable* creativity. We don't mean raw, dramatic, radical creativity that requires us to change.

So when teachers ask their classes to be creative, they want the children to take the crayons and draw on the paper, making sure that it is turned a particular way so that it will hang neatly on the wall for parents' night. Teachers certainly don't want their students to draw off the paper and down the table leg.

That mentality even applies at the university. We think of the university as the seat of creativity because it is there that we assemble our finest minds. We expect the faculty and students to operate at their creative best. But here again, we are talking about manageable creativity. It is no accident that the great achievements in human creativity, the discoveries and theories that have fundamentally reshaped our world, have come from people who at the time of their most creative acts were not at universities but were working either independently or at small, unorthodox institutions. I think of people like Einstein, Freud, Gandhi, Marx, Darwin, or Edison. These people were working either alone or in small and relatively short-lived institutions, such as Freud's Vienna Institute or Edison's laboratory. Modern art and architecture began outside the university at places like the Bauhaus, and gradually made their way in. Science itself operated for centuries outside the university, entering only about two hundred years ago.

Once a great breakthrough occurs, it is possible for the university to engage in all kinds of creative work that flows from it. University scientists did not create the science of genetics, but they did discover DNA. They did not develop the formula $E = MC^2$, but they used it to sustain the first nuclear reaction. Manageable creativity, in other words.

The university is cast in this role for good reason. Its purpose is to educate the young, to be the reservoir of our knowledge, to guard the disciplines, to stand as a bulwark against political efforts to shut down inquiry. To serve those functions, it must last, and to last it must necessarily be conservative, minimizing risk and radical change. By its very nature, it cannot embrace ideas until they are well accepted.

Organizing Differently

A similar dynamic occurs in organizations of all kinds, including business organizations. While they might like to think that they are organized for creativity, companies that are sizable and think of themselves as permanent cannot encourage creative acts as well as a new and relatively temporary organization can.

When a company wants to stimulate creativity, it may need to organize quite differently. Xerox Park, a small unit separate from the Xerox organization, became responsible for some of the most radical developments in computer engineering. At Lockheed's famous "Skunk Works," also a semi-autonomous unit, leaders like Kelly Johnson and Ben Rich developed airplanes advanced far beyond what was thought possible, including the U-2 spy plane and the stealth fighter.

Companies like Xerox and Lockheed—and now many others—have learned that scale is the enemy of creativity and are finding ways to break into more flexible units. Following that formula, even within the context of a large organization, they can provide their leaders with more latitude to follow potentially creative paths.

19

We Want for Ourselves Not What We Are Missing, but More of What We Already Have

IN MY GRADUATE school days, I worked on a small project in which I asked people to describe their ideal selves. One of the subjects in my study was an Olympic athlete, and I was intrigued that he seemed to want for himself more of what he already had: great athletic ability. Another person, a brilliant scholar, wanted more intelligence, something that was already his strong point. Over and over again in that study, I realized that people wanted for themselves not something that was missing in them—and that others might think important for them to have—but more of what was already their special attribute.

I began to see this phenomenon everywhere. People who have great beauty may say they would like to be appreciated for their other qualities, but it is their beauty to which they pay most attention. People already quite fluent in speaking will wish to be more articulate. Powerful people want more power, and so on.

When I worked with human relations groups where people described what they wanted for themselves, they seldom mentioned qualities that others would later suggest were missing from their personality or performance. A woman who was very composed and serene—and seemed to want more of that for herself—was asked if it wouldn't be important to experience more earthiness and passion and creativity to make her life more complete. A man who relied heavily on his sense of humor, quick wit, and ability to joke his way through conversations was urged to experience times when he could be serious and thoughtful and penetrating.

It was not that these two were asked to give up what they had been relying on for so long. Rather, by allowing themselves to experience other behaviors, they might enrich their lives. As Abraham Kaplan noted, "If, as Socrates said, the unexamined life is not worth living, so the unlived life is worth examining." Still, few of us are willing even to make that effort.

Danger Signs Unheeded

For years I was a member of an organization known for its work in management and human relations training. At one point in its history, this group found itself deeply in debt and worried about its ability to survive. The response of its leaders was to hire a consultant to help them, of all things, to work on the group's internal human relationships. They seemed to think that if their interpersonal relations were better, whatever troubled them would abate.

I suggested that perhaps the first order of business was to erase the debt. But my comments fell on deaf ears; they continued to put money and time into working on the human side of the enterprise. The organization, so intent on becoming more accomplished in an area where it already was highly accomplished, was failing to attend to a threat to its very existence. It very nearly went bankrupt.

In another situation, I was one of the first of many consultants to help a high-tech East Coast company institute experiments in the organization of work teams. This effort quickly captured the interest of the founder and president of the company, a technical genius from Caltech who had developed the company's leading product, which dominated the market. In fact, he became so fascinated with the success of the first work teams that he brought in additional consultants, all prominent in that field, to add their wrinkles to our efforts. The experiments seemed so successful that they were written about in business and even popular publications.

Before long, however, the company began to lose market share. But the president continued to be absorbed in the human relations side of the business. I suggested to him that in his eagerness to explore the fascinating human dimensions of the business, he may have been neglecting such areas as product diversification, relations with financial institutions, and so forth. But his emphasis on the experiments —so satisfying to him—continued, even to the point where his company came dangerously close to going under.

Setting the Stage for Trouble

The difficulty for all of us is that our absorption with what we do well may blind us to what will enable us to do even better. The particular challenge for managers is to remain mindful that organizations can set themselves up for trouble when they rely solely on the things they are already doing well and fail to see what they *really* need to do.

20

Big Changes Are Easier to Make Than Small Ones

IF EVER THERE were a godfather to the idea of management of the absurd, it would surely be C. Northcote Parkinson, author of the famed Parkinson's law, "Work expands to fill the time available." He was also responsible for many other similarly witty but powerful insights into the absurdities of human organizations.

It was Parkinson who formulated the observation that the time a committee takes to discuss an item on the agenda is inversely proportional to the amount of money involved. All who have sat through budget meetings will recognize that phenomenon. It may take hours to discuss hundred-dollar items, while million-dollar items fly by. Almost everybody knows something sensible to say about a small item on the budget, but few can offer wise comments about a million-dollar item.

The CEO of a medium-sized electronics company once told me that in one day he was able to completely change the shape of his organization, flatten the organization chart, and eliminate several levels of management—but it took days to persuade one person to move his desk ten feet. We are all painfully aware of the excessive time taken up in minor issues. Henry Kissinger is credited with the remark that the reason university faculty discussions and disputes are so time-consuming and acrimonious is that the stakes are so low.

The Case Against Gradualism

In most of our efforts to bring about change, we are counseled to take a gradual approach. The metaphor usually applied in these cases—that we must crawl before we can walk and walk before we can run—seems to make good common sense. But it may be that in the area of human affairs, that is not always the best counsel. Physician Dean Ornish, in arguing for a strict diet regimen, says that "It is easier to make big changes rather than small ones because the benefits are so much more dramatic and they occur so much more quickly."

Certainly, as we look at the pursuit of civil rights in America, it is not at all clear that gradualism has worked that well. The pace of change has certainly been gradual, but whether gradualism as a strategy has been effective is debatable. Martin Luther King called it the "tranquilizing drug of gradualism."

The bold act that most dramatically and quickly brought about racial integration in a major institution of our society was President Harry Truman's elimination of Jim Crow laws in the armed services, which he accomplished by executive order. Segregation in the military yielded not by gradualism but by massive immediate change, albeit resented and resisted.

Conversely, the gradual approach to integration has encountered resentment and resistance while failing to bring about necessary change. While it is clear that African-Americans have made significant gains since slavery, it is also true that, except in special cases, the differences between them and whites on economic and social bases have not diminished for decades. The disparity between incomes is still substantial, our communities by and large are not integrated, and racism remains a strong force.

I remember being told at the beginning of the modern civil rights movement that it might take an entire generation before the movement's overall objectives could be achieved. That was two entire generations ago, and still we see little change in the way in which African-Americans and whites live together. The big change made by Truman held; the little ones have been much easier to resist.

Bold Moves

General Motors stunned the business world in 1991 when the automaker announced that it would close twenty-one factories and lay off seventy four thousand employees. Pain ful as it was, the action perfectly illustrated the case to be made for big changes. The company's managers were convinced that downsizing had to be accomplished. They could do it one factory at a time, reaping adverse publicity and hostile employee reaction every tortuous step of the way. Or they could put it behind them as quickly as possible and move on with the business of recovery. Their success at "instant downsizing" did not go unnoticed at other major corporations, which soon were doing the same.

Chiat/Day Advertising and the Oticon Corporation of Stockholm are among the companies that have made radical changes in the design of their operations. Both used advanced communication technologies to switch to paperless systems, restructure their management, do away with private offices, and become "virtual" companies. Such radical change would be impressive even if accomplished over a fairly long period of time. But in fact, both companies accomplished the changes all at once.

If big changes are easier to make than small ones, that does not, of course, mean that making such changes is appropriate as a general strategy. Usually, not enough patient, careful analysis goes into management decisions, large or small. But the fact remains that people respect bold moves, and are more likely to buy into a change if it is big enough to withstand any attempt at countering it.

21

We Learn Not from Our Failures but from Our Successes— and the Failures of Others

How OFTEN EACH of us has said, "I'll never do that again." Or, "I'm not going to make that mistake anymore." But we do, of course, repeat over and over again the mistakes we make in school, in marriage, in work, and in life. Through it all, we continue to believe that we learn from these failures.

Conversely, we seem obsessed with the success of others. We believe that we can somehow learn from their examples. We pay a lot of money for books, lectures, and training programs produced by those whose major success is essentially in selling themselves as successes. The results are negligible, but we keep looking for success formulas.

We should probably stop looking. Most psychological theories would steer us in the other direction—toward the idea that we learn from our *own* successes. When we succeed in achieving a goal, the behavior that led us to that goal is reinforced, or "learned." When our successes are relatively consistent, our rate of learning rises accordingly. But wait. Isn't life, like baseball, mostly failure? Don't we miss a good deal more than we hit? Sure. But that doesn't mean that we learn from our failures, any more than a batter who swings at a ball and misses learns from that miss.

Nevertheless, it's important that we fail. We need to fail often. If we don't, it means we're not testing our limits. It means we're not taking the necessary risks to improve our behavior. Tennis players who never double-fault are playing the game too cautiously. Skiers who never fall are not skiing close to their capabilities. But we don't learn from those failure experiences.

Learning from success happens when, as in athletics, you are on your game, things are working for you, anything seems possible—and you are stimulated by your achievements. When we are doing a series of things right, it gives us the strength and encouragement to continue—which leads to our greatest successes. On the other hand, a series of failures can demoralize us.

Relating to Failure

While we may think we are motivated by hearing about the success of others, believe it or not, little is more encouraging or energizing than learning about or witnessing another's failure, especially if it is an expert who is failing. But there is an even stronger reason why we can learn from the failures of others, beyond the simple pleasure of knowing that an expert can fail too. It has to do with our ability as human beings to relate better to people in their failures than in their successes, and to learn more in the process.

My teacher and colleague Carl Rogers used to say that he didn't really know how to talk to people unless they were talking to him about a problem they had. At first I thought that was an unfortunate limitation in his personality. But then I came to realize that to some extent it was true for me too, that I related to people so much better when they were talking to me about their failures than about their successes.

I have since noticed this is true of people generally. Very few of us are capable of responding to another's success with the same sensitivity and wholeheartedness that we extend to that person's failure. Few of us also have the insight or the honesty of author Gore Vidal, who remarked, "Whenever a friend succeeds, a little something in me dies." But it's more than that. Responding to failure seems to bring out something good in us. It's not that we want other people to suffer; it's that we know better how to empathize with the person who is suffering than we do with a person who is succeeding. Even though we applaud and wish the best for that fortunate person, it is less easy for us to share the experience of success than to share the experience of failure.

Perhaps that's why gossip is such a unifying force. We attach to gossip the most derogatory terms, yet it is probably the single most community-building and social-bonding experience we have. Gossip seldom revolves around the description of others' successes, however, because sharing stories of others' troubles is what brings us together.

Not in Our Control

In our society, we tend to attribute success and failure to personal behavior. We like to personalize the issue, and we set up our reward systems accordingly. But most of our successes and failures are due to forces well beyond our own making and not within our control. Other societies, such as Japan, recognize this better than we do.

While we single out individuals for recognition, the Japanese are more likely to credit the group, because they know that success is seldom actually a matter of individual achievement and, moreover, they want to foster cooperative attitudes among group members.

Sometimes, success is a result of pure luck. Organizations that are enjoying a period of affluence often attribute their success to management skills, when it may be just lucky positioning in the market. Even some of the companies that are regarded as best managed owe much to luck. If the Justice Department hadn't filed an antitrust suit forcing IBM out of its founder's favorite punch-card business, IBM surely would not have become a leader in computers. The role of luck in life is greatly underrated, but be careful not to tell that to a CEO. As E. B. White noted, "Luck is not something you mention in the presence of self-made men."

I often think of a comment made to me by the late Jonas Salk, celebrated developer of the polio vaccine. In a pensive mood, he said, "I'm rebuilding my life out of the ashes of success." Success and failure are intimately connected. They are related to each other in the same way that peaks and valleys are related. They define each other. We can't have one without the other. Sometimes what seems to be a success is, in fact, failure, and vice versa. Or one leads to the other. And if success is due, at least in part, to good luck, then failure may be the result of bad luck. That is why success or failure can never be the sole measure of the accomplishments of others—or of our own accomplishments.

Could Be, Seldom Is

The idea that we learn from our failures is built on the notion that we learn from our own experience, that experience is the best teacher. In one sense that is obviously true, because experience is really all we have. But to learn from experience means that we have to process it in some way that makes it available to us. We have to analyze it. And most of us, for one reason or another, don't do that. We don't want to take the time and energy, we don't want to know the unpleasant aspects of it, we don't like to look deeply into our failures. Experience could be the best teacher, but it seldom is.

Organization consultant Robert Tannenbaum says that too many senior managers who may have been at the job thirty years don't necessarily have thirty years of experience —they have more like one year of experience, thirty times.

22

Everything We Try Works, and Nothing Works

I HAVE ALWAYS been puzzled, and I suppose disturbed, by the fact that management consultants whose approaches I disdain, who I think are not well trained or maybe even a shade unethical, seem to have more or less the same successes in their work as the consultants I most respect. That is, it seems to matter little what techniques or approaches are attempted; they all seem to work. When we put that observation together with the unsettling fact that any changes introduced by consultants will soon fade and disappear, leaving almost no trace of their having ever been instituted, we have an interesting paradox. It does seem that everything we try works, yet nothing works.

It has been a matter of some embarrassment for psychologists to live with research results that show that all schools of therapy, even those fundamentally at odds with each other, produce essentially the same results. People get better in the same proportions whether they are in psychoanalysis or hypnotherapy or any of what are now literally hundreds of other forms of treatment. But like management consulting, the effects are somehow illusory; it is very difficult to show lasting behavioral changes as a result of any of these approaches.

Unaware of that phenomenon, a management consultant may claim to have discovered the "right" way to do things after inventing a technique that seems to be well received, to be producing the desired effect. The trouble is that it doesn't make any difference what the technique is—they all work.

We see this most clearly in management training exercises, especially in the techniques used to explore human relations. There are now countless manuals crammed with such techniques. I'm sure they all work. I can even imagine the leader of a management training group just saying, "All right, I'm now going to turn off all the lights in the room so we cannot see each other as we continue to discuss the issues we were dealing with." At the end of the session, people would probably say that it was the best session they had experienced, that they had never gotten so much out of a conversation before.

Consultants or managers who have instituted training programs can easily be misled by the reaction of the work force. People will often say the most amazingly enthusiastic things about whatever method or technique they have been exposed to, especially if it has been something of an ordeal. It is not uncommon for them to say, "This has changed my life, I'll never be the same again. It's the most marvelous thing that has happened to me." Not easy words to dismiss, especially if you want very much to hear them.

No Right Way

Young managers become enthusiastic about new techniques because they have yet to learn that everything works and nothing works. That's why the worst charlatan and the most demented cult leader can have devoted followers, and why every fad captures a certain number of managers. But it certainly presents a dilemma for the responsible manager who is genuinely trying to sort things out. Studies of management are rather confusing. There appears to be no right way to be a manager.

Completely different types of leaders enjoy equal success, and part of the reason is that employees have the power to make their leaders look good. Organizations survive because most people are trying to do their best and will make an effort to keep things going under any circumstances, no matter what kind of leadership they are given. It has always puzzled researchers why a gruff, demanding autocrat could have roughly the same results as a gentle, sensitive, democratically oriented manager. Some suggest that whatever their management style, if it is authentically *theirs,* if it is congruent with them personally, it will succeed.

Others say that style is just an overlay on sound management principles: fairness, integrity, tenacity, feeling a genuine respect and even affection for the group, going to bat for its members, holding out a vision for them, working hard, demonstrating a genuine commitment to the task and to the organization. That's why managers who may be good at starting things but not good at follow-through, or good at seeing the big picture but not able to attend to detail, all can be successful. Their employees often compensate for those differences and actually make the managers succeed.

Easy Come, Easy Go

If we look at the aftermath of some of our best known management studies, we can find ample reason to doubt the seductive but deceptive idea that something is "working." Tom Peters and Robert Waterman, in their best-selling book *In Search of Excellence,* identified companies engaged in practices that had earned them excellent standing in the market. It was not long, however, before a number of these companies, which presumably were continuing their supposedly effective practices, ran into considerable difficulty and could no longer be considered "excellent."

The classic Hawthorne studies in the 1930s found that when people are paid attention to—and they believe that management's efforts are designed to help them—productivity will increase even in situations where one would expect it to decrease. The studies led to the installation of a program designed to pay more attention to workers at the Western Electric plant in Hawthorne, Illinois, site of the research. Years later, a frustrated F. J. Roethlisberger, one of the study's coauthors, told me, "It's all gone, there's nothing left." As Roethlisberger explained it, everything he and his colleague Elton Mayo had undertaken eventually was abandoned. There was no trace of the program left.

The Hawthorne studies show that it is relatively easy to produce changes in a limited, experimental situation. Yet, as we have seen from the consequences of that very experiment, it doesn't take long for those changes to disappear.

It Takes Practice

People can make lasting changes in themselves only through a commitment to a continuing discipline. For example, crash diets don't work, but a permanent modification of one's eating habits does. Visits to spas don't work (after they're over), but the daily practice of exercising, stretching, or weight lifting does. The same is true in management. Lasting change comes only from the adoption of sound management principles that are practiced on a continuing basis. There are no quick fixes.

23

Planning Is an Ineffective Way to Bring About Change

BY AND LARGE, organizations are simply not good at changing themselves. They change more often as a result of invasion from the outside or rebellion from the inside, less so as a result of planning. One could argue that it is plans, not planning, that is ineffective. Certainly, the planning process itself can be valuable. But the distinction has to do with *making change happen.* Neither plans nor planning is especially effective in that regard.

Planning is built upon the flawed idea that it is possible to predict the future. Yet the future almost always takes us by surprise. Since there is simply no good way to predict future events, there is no sure way to plan for them.

Here are some other reasons why plans and planning are of so little use in bringing about change.

The members of an organization tend to be blind to those aspects of the organization crying out for change. They often do not see what may be obvious to others. That's why it's so easy to be an expert in someone else's organization. Additionally, the organization generally has an interest in maintaining the status quo, including commitments to people and programs that may no longer be aiding the organization. Anyone charged with planning cannot help but be influenced by this reluctance to change.

The planning process tends to be located in a relatively low-status department so that the planners are not knowledgable about the organization's top-level concerns. Thus their plans cannot be truly strategic. Too often, planning is an empty ritual designed to make management feel there is something going on in that area. Plans are made but they are seldom put into use, checked and rechecked against the actual experiences of the organization. Little wonder that planners constantly feel frustrated.

The fact that planning is usually confined to one department is in itself limiting. When planning is not a function of management in all departments, there is no broad organizational "buy-in." The plans remain sterile because they have not been sold to, or had the participation of, the larger organization.

The planning process usually cannot effectively accommodate in its plans the many political pressures that are brought upon the managers charged with implementing the plans. In city planning, for example, large real-estate developers and other special-interest groups that make financial contributions to politicians are able to obtain legislation that works against the best intentions of the planners. Individual citizens who try dealing with city planning departments to get their own plans accepted may see the planners as being very powerful. But those within the department feel relatively powerless against the influence of special interests. Corporate planners can be similarly circumvented by directors who have sweetheart relationships with other corporations, by executives with pet projects that don't fit the plan, by the company's informal or even secret relationships with suppliers or competitors, and so on.

Carrying out plans to the letter ordinarily requires such authoritative control that the human spirit is stifled. Planned communities are an example of this. They are beautiful, clean, and orderly, but their inhabitants pay a price. The price when order takes precedence over vitality is the loss of individual liberty. Communities and organizations of all kinds need order. But they also need its opposite: spontaneity, a certain degree of chaos, even messiness. Just as our great cities have bohemian neighborhoods where spontaneity and creativity can thrive, organizations should make room for those aspects of human behavior that authoritarian plans would discourage.

Planning is as vulnerable to fashion as any other managerial activity. As it happens, planning is itself a fad that was much more popular a decade or so ago, when "strategic planning" was the byword of management. It is no longer the case.

Self-interest can be a barrier to effective planning. In particular, the professions stubbornly resist planned change and seem interested only in protecting themselves. If the professions actually did plan with the public interest in mind, they would probably have to merge with each other or go out of business. At the least, they would have to diversify, retrain their members, and engage in all sorts of activities that would threaten the status quo. That is why their plans are seldom ambitious or radical.

Rebellion and Invasion

Earlier, I observed that rebellion or invasion from the outside will change an organization more often than planning. The labor movement is an example of a rebellion with lasting effects. It has wrought far more fundamental change in the ways in which organizations function than has, say, the introduction of any management technique.

Similarly, the invasion of the computer is certainly changing organizations. We are now observing huge shifts in the way organizations think of themselves as a result of computerization.

Corporate takeovers, whether hostile or friendly, are another example of organizations changed dramatically by invasion—especially when new owners make major changes even before they really are a part of the reorganized company.

Given just these three developments, one would not today design an organization of the future in the same way that organizations have been designed in the past.

A Way to Make Ready

If planning is so ineffective, why do we do it? And why is it so important that we continue to do it?

Planning may not be effective at assessing the future, but it can be a good way to assess the present. It also indicates trade-offs that may be necessary, sets boundaries so that possibilities can be carefully assessed, simulates plausible scenarios, integrates ideas, and forces people to think about consequences. Additionally, it can put management on what planner Jivan Tabibian calls an "anticipatory alert," so that it is better prepared for the unexpected.

The process, not the product, is what is important. At its best, planning becomes a form of anticipatory, strategic thinking—the basis for organizational flexibility and readiness. That may be the most it can offer, but that's a lot.

24

Organizations Change Most by
Surviving Calamities

WHEN I ASK people what was most important in shaping
their lives, they often tell me of the beneficial effects of
having survived the Depression, the loss of a family member,
or a near-fatal accident. We have always honored this concept in our lore. We call it the school of hard knocks—
coping with adversity builds character. But we have a difficult
time factoring that belief into our ideas of management, and
for good reason: It presents us with the paralyzing absurdity
that the situations we try hardest to avoid in our organizations would actually be the most beneficial for them.

It is hard to imagine how surviving calamities could be
good for organizations. Yet we know that people grow and
prosper not just because of the good things that happen to
them, but perhaps even more because of the bad things, the
disasters, the crises. Such experiences often cause people to
make major reassessments of their lives and to change them
in ways that reflect a deeper understanding of their own
capabilities, values, and goals.

Organizations tend to react similarly to major adversity.
It's never easy, but they do seem to change as a result of
surviving calamities. Not all calamities can be survived, of
course. Many of them are lethal and can indeed end organizations. But like many men and women who have spent

their lives struggling and are in many ways better for it, organizations that struggle develop a sense of pulling together, ways of coping that keep them afloat where others sink.

Change by Shock Wave

Sometimes even the giant calamities that organizations suffer are beneficial. The death of a charismatic leader or founder is an example. At the time, it seems absolutely ruinous. But many organizations have reported, much to their surprise, that the loss of their great leader freed them from strictures they weren't even aware of.

A huge layoff can send a shock wave through an organization, making many wonder if it will survive. Yet about half the time, the drastic reduction in the work force rids the organization of the less effective employees and toughens the remaining force so that it actually does better. Often, executives in such situations find they are getting more work done with fewer people.

A hostile takeover of an organization may also be seen as a calamity. But while the people going through the ordeal tend to be convinced that it is a disaster from which they will never recover, the takeover often produces as much good as bad, and the resulting organization is stronger. Bankruptcy is another potentially beneficial calamity. Many organizations never survive it, but those that do often come back healthier and better able to keep focused on the important goals.

The Conventional Wisdom

Although individuals will acknowledge calamities as important in their development, managers are less likely to cite organizational calamity as the reason for change and growth.

Calamities are an embarrassment to management and not likely to be regarded as the key to success.

Managers would rather say that their *management* of the crises was crucial to success: indeed, that is the conventional wisdom. But the truth is we don't fully understand, either with respect to how individuals grow or how companies flourish, the toughening effect of plain old calamity. In any case, the absurdity remains: In management, we have no alternative but to try to avoid the very things that could be most beneficial.

25

People We Think Need Changing Are Pretty Good the Way They Are

NEWSPAPER EDITORS GRIMACE when challenged by the tired question "Why can't you ever print any good news? Why is it all trouble, disaster, crime, violence, corruption, death?" The answer, of course, is that they couldn't sell many newspapers otherwise. But the question does speak to a valid point. The consequence of news as we know it is that we develop a picture of society that does not reflect how most people actually behave.

We have little confidence that people will do the right thing because we are so often made aware of the times when they do not. Our hysteria over crime and violence in America, for example, in the face of solid evidence that for several decades both have actually declined, is understandable. The fires of fear are fanned by the media, which cannot resist putting the horror stories on the front page while the statistics about crime reduction are relegated to the inside pages, and by politicians who believe that exploiting fear is a sure road to election.

We would never know from newspapers and TV that our society is becoming more law-abiding even while it becomes more urban, complex, and rife with new laws to obey or break. We don't receive the information that might cause us to entertain what many would regard as an absurd thought—that people are pretty good the way they are.

Managers have the same problem. The workplace stories they most often hear tend to be bad news: foul-ups, delays, cheating, failures, incompetence. Not much there to make managers feel good about the people they deal with.

Business and industry respond by spending billions of dollars each year to train, encourage, and reward their employees—and to install security systems. But such efforts to fix people don't usually work, and may even be counterproductive. Situations, more than individuals, are what produce the difficulties, even though it almost always looks as if it is individuals who are fouling up.

The better managers try to fix situations, not people, by making structural changes in their organizations. Rather than attempting to change individuals, they are much more likely to change reporting relationships, enlarge or reduce the expectations of the job, set up flextime arrangements, and so on.

The fact is that we can arrange situations to make people look either bad or good. We can devise experiments where almost anyone will cheat. And we can do the opposite, where the honor system works extremely well. Circumstances are powerful determinants of behavior. Nobody smokes in church.

Finding the Ceiling

Most employees are trying to do the best they can. They prefer to do good work, to cooperate, to meet objectives. They prefer harmony over conflict, action over inaction, productivity over delays. Not everyone, and not all the time. But in general, people want to perform effectively.

Managers may have trouble recognizing this because we have never bothered to study human beings at their best, at their peak moments of achievement. Most studies of human behavior are done on people in school (a situation in which people are seldom at their best). Others are done in even less promising situations, such as clinics or prisons. Consequently, we really don't know what people are capable of doing. So our efforts are usually attempts to reform people rather than to educate, enlighten, and appreciate them, allowing their best to emerge.

The policies and practices of our organizations often reflect this demented view of human resources. I once listened as management consultant Jack Gibb asked a group of managers in an exercise to design an organization that would produce the lowest levels of trust among its employees. He wanted to know what actions they would take and what procedures they would institute to create a low-trust organization.

The managers had no trouble in generating a number of ideas: Make sure that everything is locked up. Install time clocks. Introduce voluminous manuals of operating procedures. Develop rules and regulations on everything. Fire people without warning. Keep thick personnel folders on people to which they have no access. Hold private meetings to which most people are not admitted. And so on. One by one, the managers in the audience flushed with embarrassment and amusement as they recognized that they were describing aspects of their own organizations.

When Gibb reversed the exercise and asked his audience to invent a high-trust organization based upon the idea that human nature is not all that bad, the managers tended to generate maxims that sounded very much like what is typically taught as good management practice: Take care to explain matters fully. Reverse the flow of communication. Develop a set of shared goals. Build a team rather than concentrating only on individuals. Offer rewards rather than punishment. Stay in touch with what is happening on the floor. Pay attention to the concerns, issues, and personal problems of the employees. Enlarge people's jobs.

In short, what flows naturally from a belief in the positive side of human nature is just sound management, and the positive approach can become just as self-fulfilling as the negative.

Psychology professor Michael Kahn has demonstrated how setting ground rules for group behavior in seminars can elicit high achievement. He points out that most seminars are organized like beauty contests, in which people are encouraged to show off their individual abilities and to appear smart when compared to others in the group. So it becomes important to them not only to look good themselves, but to criticize and even undermine others in the group.

In his seminars, Kahn tries to achieve what he calls "barn raising," an approach built on the metaphor of pioneer days, when people who needed a new barn could count on their friends and neighbors to help build it. Instead of criticizing each other's ideas, he encourages people to try to advance them. The group takes someone's thought and attempts to build on it, to see if it really will become a structure worth saving. Although the approach may be very different from what people are used to, it is surprisingly easy to enter into once the ground rules are established. The resulting discussion is always more productive.

The Way We Are

Most of us regret things we have done in our lives, and continue to rehash episodes in our minds that we wish we had handled differently. But by and large, when we look back most of us probably wouldn't want to change much. This is because one's life is made up of a full range of experiences, the good things often dependent upon the bad, and vice versa.

The same holds true for organizations. When we build a team of people, we may, at the outset, wish that its members were different from what they are—we think this one might be too shy, that one too boisterous, another too cerebral, and so on. But once the team is built and begins working together, something pleasantly surprising happens. Instead of continuing to want to change these people, all those characeristics that may have concerned us at the outset become qualities we come to appreciate as simply being part of the way these people are. Absurdly, we find that we really wouldn't want it any other way.

PART SEVEN

The Aesthetics of Leadership

26

Every Great Strength Is a Great Weakness

OFTEN WHEN WE want to assess others, or even ourselves, we make lists of characteristics. On one side of the paper we write down strengths, and on the other side weaknesses. But we really need a list in the middle for those strengths that are also weaknesses, and those weaknesses that are also strengths. Because of the fundamental duality of human experience, the list in the middle will tell us more than the other lists.

Strengths can become weaknesses when we rely too much on them, carry them to exaggerated lengths, or apply them where they don't belong. The stronger they are, the more likely they are also to be weaknesses. For example, people who have great critical and intellectual powers, who win every argument, may overrely on those strengths. In so doing, they leave themselves no room for an emotional response and often run roughshod over the ideas and opinions of others.

People who are exceptionally beautiful or handsome may fail to build up other qualities—for example, working hard to learn skills or become educated.

People who are tenacious sometimes continue that behavior long after it has become evident that they should change course or give up.

People who are extremely careful about dieting sometimes need to relax and break a few rules.

People who are self-critical and self-demanding may need to be more self-accepting and kinder to themselves.

People who are extraordinarily successful find that success often separates them from others.

We add the phrase "to a fault" in describing such characteristics in individuals: he is generous to a fault, she is loyal to a fault, and so forth. While we all can appreciate the charm in the late New York socialite Barbara Paley's famous comment, "One cannot be too thin or too rich," we're also well aware that it is entirely possible to be too thin or even too rich.

On the Other Hand

If strengths are also weaknesses, is the reverse true? Can a weakness be a strength? Very often the answer is yes. Fearfulness can serve us well, sometimes making us appropriately cautious. Perfectionists can be among our most valuable workers. Feelings of inadequacy lead to the need to achieve. Hypochondriacs take better care of their health. An obsessive, single-minded executive can inspire others.

As a psychologist, I used to believe the conventional wisdom that in order to see others clearly I needed to see myself clearly—to be psychologically healthy myself. It is for that reason that psychotherapists are ordinarily required to undergo extensive therapy for themselves as part of their training. But I am suspicious of the idea now.

So many brilliant leaders in my field are, in their own personal dealings, extremely difficult individuals who are clearly in less than optimal psychological health. Yet they demonstrate an uncanny ability to read other people quickly and with great understanding.

I now believe that such people exemplify a terrible weakness that is also a great strength. Many giants of psychology have extraordinary abilities not in spite of, but because of, their own emotional disabilities. Experiences in their lives that have led them to be uncomfortable with others have taught them to read people quickly and carefully, because others have always represented a potential threat. Those of us who grew up under healthier circumstances just don't need to make quick assessments of others, because we simply didn't learn to fear them.

Two Companies, Same Paradox

Weight lifters can accomplish remarkable feats of strength. But they are so muscle-bound that they do not have the quickness of gymnasts. On the other hand, gymnasts have agility but lack the strength of the weight lifters.

That weight lifter/gymnast dichotomy characterizes the difficulty two highly regarded firms encountered when they attempted to enter the personal computer market. IBM, the heavyweight of computer companies, maker of the most popular mainframes, deep with professional talent, doing business in more than 150 countries, was unable to compete as successfully as it might have in the personal computer market, because turning a company the size of IBM is like turning an ocean liner.

KayPro, on the other hand, was small and family owned. The company was led by the electronic genius who had designed its highly successful digital voltmeter, a device that commanded more than half the market. Now a personal computer was in the works. In an amazingly short time, this agile company completed the design, entered the consumer electronic market, and went public. But although it was agile, KayPro lacked the size, experience, and depth of professional management to compete effectively with the giants in the field.

Today, both IBM and KayPro compete in the personal computer market, but with decidedly less market share than would have been possible had their strengths not also been weaknesses.

Check the Clothing

So it is helpful for organizations to be aware that when they rely solely on what has become their strength, they can seriously err. One company deals sensitively with its human relations—but to the exclusion of other vital activities, such as researching new markets or developing new technologies. Another dominates a market—and becomes complacent and inflexible. Yet another company, noted for its commitment to its people, has difficulty in cutting back and getting lean in order to compete more effectively. Strengths and weaknesses come dressed in the same clothing.

27

Morale Is Unrelated to Productivity

IT IS COMMONLY assumed by managers that morale is the chief factor in motivating people to work hard. But that may not be so.

In fact, people tend to work hard for many different reasons. They were brought up that way, taught the work ethic. They have an inner drive, sometimes even an addiction to the narcotic of work. They want greater wealth. They are driven by family pressures, by fear. They feel challenged by job enlargement, promotions, or new responsibilities. They love their jobs. In short, there are a good many important reasons why people work hard that have little to do with morale.

Most managers associate "morale" with a happy and satisfied work force, and it is in this sense that I believe morale to be clearly unrelated to productivity. Searching the dictionary definition of "morale," we do not find the words "happiness" or "satisfaction." But even my dictionary's definition —"a confident, resolute, willing, often self-sacrificing and courageous attitude of an individual"—may be equally unrelated to productivity, as absurd as that may seem.

We have to distinguish between what it is that makes people work hard and what accounts for productivity. Hard work is only a small part of productivity.

We Do and Don't Want Productivity

Not that productivity is any organization's main objective, even in America. When it comes down to a choice between productivity and any number of other values and behaviors —such as maintaining the status quo or holding on to one's stereotypes—it becomes immediately apparent that productivity is seldom our paramount goal. If we were interested only in productivity we would, for example, find ways of making better use of women, who represent more than half of our talent, and better use also of people at both ends of the age spectrum.

We want productivity only if there is little cost in terms of changing our ideas, only if it makes life easier. We keep people in an organization at a level of motivation, productivity, and creativity that is nonthreatening. In companies that pay employees not for their time but for their productivity, serious conflict can be caused by those who work so fast that they make others look slow. Such employees, called "rate busters" because their efforts can result in lowered rates paid for piecework, have always been isolated and punished by other workers. If we really wanted productivity above all, it would come at the price of changing some of our most cherished views about how human affairs work.

The people Abraham Maslow chose for his studies of what he called self-actualization—those remarkable people who were among the greatest achievers in our society—were not necessarily comfortable or happy. They could be ruthless, boring, stuffy, irritating, and humorless. Organizations are absolutely dependent upon such people. Often the challenge of management is to make it possible for them to survive and prosper in the organizational environment.

Doing It for the Right Reasons

Management literature frequently suggests that managers take the time to bring little gifts, hold parties, recognize birthdays, send notes, and perform similar other acts of goodwill toward their employees. Not just in the hope that such gestures will make for a more productive work force, but because they help create the climate of caring that we all want for ourselves and each other. When there is genuine feeling behind such expressions and activities, and when they are undertaken for their own sake, they are certainly desirable in any organization.

But what about managers who are more calculating, who court employee favor as a morale-raising strategy? Implicit in this kind of behavior is the fallacious idea that even though they may not like someone, the managers can behave in such a way that their employees will like them. This inauthentic approach will probably fail. The better managers reverse the notion, and instead behave so that their respect for employees will grow. They recognize the paradox that it is more important for them to like their employees than for their employees to like them.

We all tend to like people we do things *for* more than people we do things *to*, or people who only do things for us. And we like people more when we do not feel victimized by them. That's why better managers can do both: be generous with their time and energy, and yet be quick to confront an employee whose behavior is victimizing. They realize that the problem is not in raising the morale of the work force; if anything, it is in raising their *own* morale as managers. If their morale is high, eventually they are more likely to develop a more creative and enthusiastic work force.

28

There Are No Leaders, There Is Only Leadership

ONE OF THE great enemies of organizational effectiveness is our stereotypical image of a leader. We imagine a commanding figure perhaps standing in front of an audience, talking, not listening, with an entourage of assistants standing by. Or sitting behind a large clean desk, barking out orders, taking charge—aggressive, no-nonsense, a bulldog.

Such images of leaders get us into trouble not just because they fail to conform to reality, but because they set us up for roles that are ultimately dysfunctional. The macho image of leadership, associated with men like Vince Lombardi, Ross Perot, and Lee Iacocca, makes us forget that the real strength of a leader is the ability to elicit the strength of the group.

This paradox is another way of saying that leadership is less the property of a person than the property of a group. Leadership is distributed among members of a group, and they in turn play such vital roles as taskmaster, clown, mother figure, and so on. Relying on one person—the manager, for example—to provide all the leadership builds expectations that cannot be met. Moreover, it robs the group of its powers, leading to overdependence on the manager. In turn, the leader's response to this dependence is sometimes to micromanage, getting into areas of control and responsibility that represent a poor use of time and may far exceed his or her capabilities, actually reducing the productivity of the group.

Defined by the Group

People who are leaders in one situation usually are followers in others. For example, they may be managers at work but just interested parents at a PTA meeting, or mere spectators at social gatherings. Leadership is situational, less a personal quality than specific to a situation.

True leaders are defined by the groups they are serving, and they understand the job as being interdependent with the group. We have all seen leaders who successfully move from one organization to another even though they may not be expert in the second organization's business. They are able to do this because they define their task as evoking the knowledge, skills, and creativity of those who are already with the organization. They are secure enough in their own identities to be able to be influenced by new information and to accept the ideas of others in the group. They are especially able to elicit the intelligence and participation of group members who otherwise might not join the discussions.

In a well-functioning group, the behavior of the leader is not all that different from the behavior of other responsible group members. In fact, if it were not for the trappings of titles, private corner offices, desks with overhangs, a seat at the head of the table, and so on, it might be difficult to identify the leader in a group that is working well.

Making Life Easier

The best leaders are servants of their people. I once conducted a study aimed at trying to understand how people achieve power in a group. We found that those people who were most successful in achieving power did not dominate the group; rather, they served it. They would go to the blackboard and perform what might be thought of as secretarial tasks for the group. They would call on those who had not spoken; they listened attentively to everyone. They spoke their own views clearly and fully, but mostly they encouraged others to speak theirs. They helped the group to stay focused on the problem. In other words, they tried to serve the group.

Humility comes naturally to the best leaders. They seldom take credit themselves but instead give credit to the group with which they have worked. They characteristically make life easier for their employees. They are constantly arranging situations, engineering jobs, smoothing out the processes, removing the barriers. They think about who needs what. They define their job as finding ways of releasing the creative potential that exists within each individual employee and in each group with which they work.

Because so much of the work of a manager is as a servant, a counselor, a confidant, it is surprising that there are not more women in these jobs, since such functions are often associated with women's traditional roles. Were it not for the unfortunate image of leader as dominator rather than servant, we probably would find more women at the top.

Leaders We Don't Recognize

We forget sometimes that leadership is a shared role played partly by people who are not titular leaders. Kings have regents whispering in their ears. Presidents have advisers. CEOs have consultants. Managers have assistants who help shape their behavior but who do not take the risks of leadership and who do not get the credit.

Indeed, leaders are themselves often led and managed by their employees, from the bottom up—colleagues whose ideas, assistance, arguments, and sometimes dogged resistance have real influence. Watching an accomplished executive secretary at work can make one wonder sometimes just who is managing whom.

I have found that there are two kinds of good employees. One is the willing assistant prepared to accept whatever tasks are assigned and to accomplish them with dispatch and good will. The other goes further, anticipating what the needs are going to be and then offering solutions, not problems, ideas, not complaints. This anticipatory role is seldom asked for; nevertheless, it is an important leadership role played by those who are not called leaders.

The Most Powerful Force

Most of the actions of leaders don't work, just as most surfers miss more waves than they catch. To complicate matters, there are so many different kinds and styles of leadership, and the actions called for are so complex, that there is no sure model to follow.

Yet leadership is the most powerful force on earth. Arguments can be made for other forces—greed, territoriality, guilt, fear, hate, love, spirituality—but without leadership to mobilize them, they are relatively weak. Leadership, therefore, deserves a great deal more attention than it has been given, especially if we want to make certain that it is exercised in ways that help our organizations thrive and our civilization progress.

29

The More Experienced the
Managers, the More They Trust
Simple Intuition

THE ONE QUALITY that many top executives agree separates
them from their less successful competitors is confidence in
their intuition. Companies will pay highly for executives with
reputations for "golden guts," whose immediate visceral reactions to people and events seem accurate, thus making
their judgments more valuable.

Most analysts would argue that what is attributed by these
executives to intuition is more likely the accumulation of
many learning experiences that have sensitized them, making them able to read situations quickly. But because the
processes the leaders go through in exercising their judgments are mysterious to them, they attribute their powers
to intuition. Notwithstanding this reasonable explanation,
there is still much to be said for the ability to trust one's own
immediate reactions.

I was once appointed dean of a school of environmental
design at a distinguished institution that housed all of the
arts, an unusual appointment for a psychologist. Understandably, I felt quite amateurish when I sat in on the selec-
tion process, reviewing the portfolios of prospective
students. I tried my best to apply what little understanding I

had of form and composition, but it seemed to take forever. What always amazed me was how quickly the other deans and faculty members who sat in on these sessions could make their judgments. They seemed to know immediately which were the better portfolios.

As time went by, I came to a startling realization. I, too, had known almost immediately which were the stronger works. But because I lacked confidence, I felt obliged to apply formal principles to the assessment process. I had been afraid to trust my own judgment, my own first reactions. I should have known this because the same phenomenon applies in psychotherapy. The most experienced therapists trust their immediate visceral reactions over complicated analytical thinking.

A Clear-Eyed Wisdom

We admire children for their quick and uninhibited judgments. To a great extent, we want to recover for ourselves the immediacy of childhood reactions. While the judgments of children may not actually be better than ours, we do nevertheless believe that they have a clear-eyed reaction to people and events, unfettered by the process of intellectualization. We attribute the same powers to animals, suggesting that Rover can always spot a bad person by the degree to which he avoids or warms up to that person. This can be seen very clearly in the ridiculous, but nevertheless compelling, formula for television programs such as *Lassie*, where the wife is always seen as wiser than the husband, the children wiser than the mother, and the animals wiser than the children. But as we get older and more experienced, we somehow lose touch with this primitive wisdom. Perhaps it is because much has happened to us as adults that has not yet happened to children, causing our judgment to be impaired.

Perhaps we learn not to see. Anthropologist Margaret

Mead told me once that children see events that we adults have learned not to notice. What this says is that experience is not always the best teacher. Sometimes it closes us down. We learn many things that blind us and lead us to mistakes in judgment.

What Gets in the Way

How are we fooled? What happens that creates barriers to good judgment? Here are some probable answers.

Both in school and at home we are taught a reliance on authority, on the opinions of others. We are taught not to trust our emotions, that our emotions are our enemies and will get us into trouble.

As adults we are often victimized by images. We learn to be impressed by résumés, by clothes, by appearances, and we tend to attribute powers and qualities to people that go well beyond reality. The ancient Greeks believed that if you were beautiful on the outside you were probably beautiful on the inside as well, that virtue and beauty went hand in hand. As Gloria Steinem points out, we may have reversed that notion in modern culture, if we believe that a beautiful woman probably isn't very bright. Both, of course, are stereotypes that blind us to the truth.

We have selective perception when it comes to supporting our belief systems. We simply ignore things that don't fit and accept things that do. We tend to find what we are looking for. Scientists usually find what they have hypothesized, politicians hear more clearly the concerns of those who share their convictions, members of religious groups see their views as being more widely held than is actually the case, those who believe in UFOs or angels are more likely to see them. Evidence to support one's beliefs is remarkably easy to find.

We are influenced by what has worked for us before. We always want to repeat our successes, even if what we did before may not apply in the current situation.

We have been taught to be suspicious of our initial reactions. We lack confidence in our first impressions because we are so often reminded of when we have made mistaken judgments that way. But actually, we learn a great deal about a person in the first few seconds of an encounter, and our first impressions are usually right. There is an often-cited psychological experiment in which people were shown photographs of faces and asked to match them with occupations from an accompanying list. Because the bank robber was more often identified as the bank president, this experiment is presented to show how wrong our first impressions can be. But if we look at all the judgments that were made of the faces, the people in the experiment tended to be correct more often than not. We have amazing abilities to assess other people. We are aware of how many times we have been embarrassingly wrong, but we don't even notice how many times we have been right.

Since it is difficult to trust our intuition when we are insecure and afraid to take risks, we feel obliged at those times to make a rational, defensible justification for our judgments. This is in contrast to what parents often do when they answer a child's question by saying simply "Because." "Why can't I?" "Because." "Why did you do that?" "Because." The word that seems to carry no meaning actually carries a great deal of meaning. It says, "My accumulated experience here has convinced me of something that I can't explain to you in rational terms, or that you cannot yet understand. I feel it deeply from head to toe, but cannot and will not take the time now to try to analyze it in terms that would do full justice to the power of the feeling I have." Too bad that an executive could never get away with answering, "Because."

Children look at things we turn away from. They will point at a person who has no legs when we wish they would ignore that person as we adults try to do. But better executives have this childlike quality of being able to wade into areas others avoid. Sometimes just pointing at what is going on is a valuable way to break through a barrier.

We are sometimes overdependent on the judgments of others. We demonstrate what psychologist Irving Janis called *groupthink,* wanting to go along with the group. Some of the greatest leadership blunders of history have come about in that way; Watergate is only one of the most recent. Many psychological experiments have shown how our perceptions can be shaped by group behavior. We actually see things differently when we are being pressured toward group consensus.

Leader as Litmus Paper

For these reasons, much of the job of executive development is an *unlearning* process—getting rid of barriers to perception and wisdom and judgment.

Leaders need to regain trust in gut reactions. To do that, we can think of ourselves as sensitive instruments, measuring situations and registering visceral reactions that are usually ignored but should be paid attention to. It's not unlike dipping litmus paper into a solution to get a reaction.

Of course, we cannot lose sight of all the rational factors that make for good decisions. While we are paying attention to our gut reactions, at the same time we must be alert for objective information that might contradict those reactions. So it can be a bit of a dilemma to judge how much value to place on visceral reactions. And when one considers the various barriers described above, it is perhaps understandable that most managers err in the direction of dismissing what their guts are telling them.

30

Leaders Cannot Be Trained, but They Can Be Educated

MUCH AS WE would like to believe that leadership is a matter of acquired expertise, there really are no expert leaders. There are good leaders, even great leaders, but they are not "expert." That is, they do not know how they got to be good, or what they do that makes them good. Ask top leaders what constitutes their leadership, and the banality of their answers persuades one that they understand little about what they do that sets them apart.

It is probably much to the good, however, that leadership is not a matter of expertise, and that the people we care most about are not expert in their relationship to us. After all, we would not want "expert" friends. There are no "friendship skills." Nor would we want expert husbands, or wives, or lovers, or parents.

But if leadership is not a matter of expertise, if the management of human relations is not a matter of skill and technique, then presumably it cannot be improved through training. What then might improve it? The answer is education.

Different Outcomes

What's the difference? Aren't these terms used almost inter-changeably? Yes, but there is an important distinction be-tween training and education in human relations. The distinction implies very different outcomes.

Training, as we know, leads to the development of skills and techniques. Each new technique implicitly reinvents the manager's job by adding a new skill requirement, a new definition of the task, and a new burden of responsibility. That is, each new technique increases the area of control for which managers feel responsible. For example, if we teach a manager techniques for handling employees troubled by drug use, that manager will almost certainly feel a new re-sponsibility for these employees' well-being, and thus this training adds an entirely new element to the manager's job description. But because techniques don't work well in human relations, the manager is often unable to adequately discharge these new-felt responsibilities. That's where the trouble comes. When people feel responsible for handling some situation in which they are, in fact, largely helpless, a dangerous combination of feelings is created: responsiblity plus helplessness leads to abuse.

We see this overburdening of role responsibilities not just in management but education, medicine, and parenthood. And we see the consequent mistreatment. When teachers cannot get their students to learn, when physicians cannot cure their patients, when parents cannot control their chil-dren, they usually do not become compassionate. They be-come abusive. The same is true for managers. Saddled with responsibilities created by the growing body of management techniques, managers who now feel frustrated and helpless resort to confrontation, argument, insult, and even more demanding and abusive measures to bring under control situations that were never possible to control.

Education, on the other hand, leads not to technique but to information and knowledge, which in the right hands can lead to understanding, even to wisdom. And wisdom leads to humility, compassion, and respect—qualities that are fundamental to effective leadership.

Training makes people more alike, because everyone learns the same skills. Education, because it involves an examination of one's personal experience in the light of an encounter with great ideas, tends to make people different from each other. So the first benefit of education is that the manager becomes unique, independent, the genuine article.

With the right kind of education, managers can gain better self-understanding, learn about their own interpersonal styles, their reactions to and impact on others, prejudices and blind spots, strengths and weaknesses. A better understanding of themselves and of their feelings gives all managers added trust in their perceptions, reactions, impulses, and instincts. If any one thing can be said to be true about good leaders, it is that they trust their instincts.

The Visionary Host

With education comes a better understanding of the context in which one's decisions are imbedded, a better perspective for viewing human affairs, and a better idea of what is important. This can lead to vision, another quality of leadership that characterizes top executives.

Education also helps leaders appreciate the aesthetics of leadership. Managers then take pleasure not only in the effectiveness of their actions, but in the gracefulness of their efforts. They become like good hosts at a party, making certain that everything works smoothly, taking care of the little things that make the experience a good one, mindful of what is going on in the interpersonal underworld, aware of the people who are on the margins of the party and need to be brought in, buffering difficult relationships, and seeing to it that everyone gets to be seen at his or her best.

Finally, and probably most important of all, education gives managers new ways of thinking, new perspectives. It can enable them to see the interconnectedness of events, to go beyond the conventional wisdom—in short, to think strategically. That process is always easier if they appreciate the pervasive role of paradox and absurdity in human affairs.

31

In Management,
to Be a Professional
One Must Be an Amateur

THE LATE DESIGNER George Nelson, who had studied with the great American architect Frank Lloyd Wright, told me an anecdote that has stayed with me. It seems that George and his famous mentor were walking together and Wright was trying to describe what he thought architecture was all about. At one point, Wright gestured toward a flower and said, "You know, George, architecture is like this flower." Then he stopped: "No, that's not it." He walked a little farther, then turned, looked back at George, and said, "Architecture is like being in love."

George told me that story more than twenty years ago, and when he finished he said, "Dick, I hope it doesn't take you as long as it took me to figure out what he meant." I'm afraid that it did, but I'm finally beginning to catch on to its meaning, not just in architecture but in all worthwhile pursuits. Let me try to explain.

Amateurs and Love

Amateurism is what makes managers give so much of themselves to their jobs; it's what gives them such a fondness for their jobs, even when those jobs are difficult, stressful, and frustrating. The best leaders make their organizations places where their passion becomes the organizing force.

"Amateur" stems from the Latin word *amator,* which means "lover." Amateurs do what they do out of love. That is a word that does not often arise in conversations about management development, yet love is fundamental to good leadership, because leadership is all about caring.

Indeed, caring is the basis for community, and the first job of the leader is to build community, a deep feeling of unity, a fellowship. Community is one of the most powerful yet most fragile concepts in the building of organizations. Community is difficult to build and easy to destroy. We see around us every day the steady erosion of community. It is perhaps the most serious trouble we face, not just locally but nationally and even globally.

One of the great dilemmas is that the erosion of community almost always happens in the name of progress. We see this perhaps most clearly with the growth of large, impersonal shopping malls and the like, but we also see it in the growth of giant corporations. One aspect of human development that social scientists have never been able to cope with is the problem of scale. Once the human organization gets to be large-scale, it is difficult to make it work as effectively as it did when it was smaller.

That is the reason for the current move to more entrepreneurial organizations. There are those who feel that the future of organizations will be in a reversion to small units because, for one thing, only in smaller units are the bonds holding people together affectional rather than simply functional, and affection is the basis of community. For example, only prisons housing fewer than twenty inmates are likely to be rehabilitative.

High Arts, Great Moments

Perhaps we need a way to define leadership that goes beyond our traditional utilitarian values into the realm of the aesthetic. We need to be able to appreciate good management for its grace and beauty.

Management and leadership are high arts. When they are working well, they compare favorably to the other great aesthetic moments of our lives, to symphonies and sunsets. These great moments of leadership burn brightly for an instant—deeply satisfying, sensuous, involving pure feeling. They may not last, but they are enriching in the same way that other aesthetic experiences are enriching.

So the good leader must be both a professional and an amateur. The professional conforms to technical and ethical standards requiring a high level of proficiency based on sound knowledge and conscientiousness. But the amateur performs work out of love, out of sensuous pleasure in the act of accomplishment, in the creation of community, in the bonds of compassion that unite.

Let me adapt for our purposes here Frank Lloyd Wright's statement that architecture is like being in love. I would say to you that leadership is like being in love. I'm sure it won't take you as long as it took me to figure that out.

PART EIGHT

Avoiding the Future

32

Lost Causes Are the Only Ones Worth Fighting For

IN A FAMOUS Frank Capra movie from the thirties, *Mr. Smith Goes to Washington,* James Stewart plays a young man just elected to the U.S. Senate. Before leaving for Washington he is encouraged by his father, who offers this paradoxical advice: "Lost causes are the only ones worth fighting for." That absurd line has stuck in my mind all these years, and I think that only now am I beginning to understand its meaning.

Lost causes are the ones most worth fighting for because they tend to be the most important, most humane ones. They require us to live up to the best that is in us, to perfect ourselves and our world. Lost causes cannot be won, but because they are so crucial to us, we nevertheless must try.

On several occasions while consulting with organizations, I have asked groups if they could identify "lost causes" in their work, goals that they were pretty sure they could not reach. Each time I was surprised to find how easy it was to elicit a response, and how enjoyable the process was. Instead of being depressed or discouraged by recalling intractable problems or stubborn associates or out-of-reach objectives that had so frustrated them, the group members seemed relieved, even exhilarated. Often they would break up in laughter as together they recognized for the first time the absurdity of efforts that had absorbed so much of their time.

An even bigger surprise for me, however, was that identifying these "lost causes" did not necessarily lead to their abandonment. Instead, the members of the group simply shared the realistic appraisal that their expectations could not be met, and then set about to work on them anyway. They did this, of course, because, impossible as they seemed, these were the tasks that meant the most to them.

Increasingly, I am guided in my own work as a consultant by the advice (when I can remember to give it to myself) that I should give up before I start. Whenever I have the arrogance or audacity to believe that I can reform people, I get nowhere. But when I fundamentally recognize that I cannot possibly accomplish those reforms, I can move ahead with a more humble posture and, paradoxically, perhaps then there is a chance that the situation can change. The absurd lesson is to recognize that it is a lost cause and work on it anyway.

Valley of the Absurd

A senior scientist at a well-known university agricultural research laboratory once described to me how he comes to grips with absurdity. The people in his organization sell ideas to industry and government, and it is his task to see if the ideas will work. Not surprisingly, they often strike him as absurd—growing plants in seawater, greening the deserts, and the like. Instead of throwing up his hands, however, he goes ahead as if each were possible. He copes with the feeling that the idea is absurd and yet acts anyway.

In his words, it is as if he descends into a deep valley (the Valley of the Absurd, he calls it), until he reaches the peaceful security of the valley floor. There, he can move about effectively. When it is time to leave, he climbs back up, returning to his regular life, ready to work on what he had earlier regarded as absurd.

In that metaphor it seems to me that he captures the essence of coping with absurdity. To dramatize it a bit, I would say that he has (1) allowed the enormity of the situation to wash over him in all its irrationality, (2) embraced the absurdity, even though he could not fully comprehend it, (3) fallen prostrate before its overwhelming complexity, giving up before he starts, and (4) then, calling upon the deep reservoir of will, discipline, experience, creativity, and even playfulness that lies within, picked himself up and started anyway, still respectful, in one corner of his mind, of the fundamental absurdity that he first recognized.

Leaving Rake Marks

If absurdity is ubiquitous, if the most important goals are lost causes, why do we keep playing this absurd game? We play it because it is the only game in town. Of course it is absurd. Of course it is only a game. But it is a game well worth playing—and worth playing well.

I was once consulting with a large government organization that manages parks. The men who had the job of cleaning campgrounds were complaining to me that they not only had to pick up under the picnic tables, which they were quite willing to do, but were told to rake under the tables as well.

I wasn't quite sure what they meant by that, so I asked, "You mean that after the area is all picked up, your supervisors want you to leave rake marks under the tables?"

They answered, "Yeah, that's it. They want us to leave rake marks!"

I was just about to agree that it was perhaps an absurd request, when I stopped and thought to myself, "I'll bet the people who do that job best leave rake marks." Now, what could be less important than leaving rake marks? But, then again, what could be more important than leaving rake marks?

Leaving rake marks has since become an important metaphor for me. It has to do with going beyond the necessary to the desirable, beyond what is required to what is elegant, beyond the purely functional to the aesthetic. Management may be a lost cause—impossible, absurd—but I know that I want very much to play that game with the best of them. I care very much about doing it right, even though I know that in the most important aspects, there is no way to be sure what "right" is.

So maybe it is key for all leaders and managers to fight for lost causes, and at the same time keep doing the "unimportant" tasks well—leaving rake marks, as it were. Maybe we all can indeed learn from the cleanup man. For while he cannot directly affect the picnickers by leaving rake marks, somehow, by doing this unimportant task well, he may, in some indirect way, help them to be better, happier people. Maybe he even helps himself.

33

My Advice Is Don't Take My Advice

ADVICE IS CHEAP, so the old adage goes. It means that not only is advice worth little, it also costs nothing to give. It is the simplest, quickest response to make when confronted with a problem. It addresses a situation without actually dealing with it. It is easier than understanding, than listening and analyzing. We know this intuitively: most of us give ourselves good advice every day but seldom act upon it. As the old farmer told the young government agricultural agent: "Son, I already know how to be twice as good a farmer as I am."

My exploration of the paradoxes of leadership is deliberately meant not to provide advice but to deepen understanding of the issues that managers face every day. In fact, I would be disappointed if the precepts presented in these pages were perceived as advice. They don't work that way.

An Invitation to Reflect

First of all, these precepts, taken at face value, would lead us to behave in a manner quite the opposite from what we have been taught all our lives, from what we are expected to do, and what we really can't help doing—even if we try not to. When I say, "Praising people does not motivate them," the advice one might infer would be "Don't praise people."

That, of course, is not what I mean. Besides, it would be impossible to follow. Try it. You probably couldn't resist the impulse to praise for even an hour. Even if it were desirable to avoid praising people, it is behavior too deeply engrained in us to change much.

Second, because my paradoxical precepts are also true in their opposite, it's difficult to know when we should act upon one, or the other. When I say that we should communicate less or that technology always backfires, I don't mean that we shouldn't communicate or use technology. We must consider both sides of these precepts at once to arrive at a fuller understanding of the consequences of our potential actions. When I say that we should keep an eye on the invisible, or that once you find a management technique that works, give it up, or that the best thing for people is to experience a calamity, I am setting up a somewhat impossible situation to challenge your thinking.

In some instances, my precepts seem selfish or perhaps even immoral. Keep your own morale high. Do things that will make you like other people, rather than make them like you. Is that advice? I think of it rather as an invitation to analyze more closely your own motivation and the complexities of your relationships with others.

But the basic reason why my precepts are impossible to translate into simple advice is that changing one's approach to leadership and organizational life is not that easy. Faced with the absurd, managers either change from a profound understanding of a new way of thinking about these issues, or they don't. Some things can't be achieved by going through the motions, and developing a genuine appreciation for the paradoxical nature of human affairs is one of them. You have to reflect on it. Only then will it become a valuable adjunct to your own leadership style.

In Support of Thinking

Most management books close with suggestions for what the manager should do differently, usually presented as formulas or checklists of actions to take. We are, after all, an action-oriented society, managers particularly. But there will be no such prescriptions for action here. As I'm sure you've gathered by now, I regard any demand for action as part of the problem, not the solution.

What we need when confronting a problem or a predicament is not quick action based upon a first glimpse, but rather a careful consideration of all the issues involved, no matter how paradoxical or absurd. Such a process can lead to a new perspective on the nature of genuine leadership. "Doing" should follow thinking, even though that thinking may make us uncomfortable because it is riddled with so many paradoxes and dilemmas. Perhaps it is more like "stewing" than thinking.

Therefore I deliberately end here, not with advice, but by returning to the unresolved paradoxes that truly characterize the human condition.

Waking Up Ludwig

In music, there is a very common sequence of chords known as the *two-five-one* sequence, referring to the second, fifth, and first notes in a scale. When the chords are played in this sequence on a piano, the listener experiences a feeling of comfortable closure when the third and final chord is played. If, however, only the first two are played, the listener experiences a tension that comes from the sequence's not being completed.

Legend has it that Frau von Beethoven, Ludwig's mother, used to wake him up when he was a little boy by playing *two-five* and not then playing the final *one* chord. Even though asleep, he would experience that missing chord and become so disturbed that he would have to get up to complete the sequence.

With my book ending at this point, you may feel a bit like little Ludwig. Perhaps that is appropriate, however, because the next notes are yours to play.

Acknowledgments

THIS BOOK HAS been forming in my mind for a number of years, and many people have helped along the way. I am grateful to them all, but here I will be able to thank only a few.

In the introduction I mentioned my great indebtedness to Carl Rogers and Alex Bavelas. I cannot imagine that I would have written this book had I not known them. Several other valued colleagues, past and present, contributed to my thinking about the paradoxical nature of human events. I remember particularly Abraham Kaplan, Gregory Bateson, Rollo May, Paul Lloyd, Michael Kahn, Mary Douglas, Don Jackson, Jonas Salk, Jivan Tabibian, Charles Hampden-Turner, and Abraham Maslow.

I would also like to express my appreciation to the several dozen leaders from different countries who participated in a computer teleconference I conducted on this subject for the International Leadership Forum of the Western Behavioral Sciences Institute. Their stimulating and thoughtful responses helped ready my own ideas for publication.

Several others deserve special thanks: Lynne Robinson, my longtime associate, for her assistance, support, and wise counsel throughout the book's preparation; Andrea Lawrence-Stuart, who worked tirelessly to type and help organize the first draft and whose advice I value greatly; Hallock Hoffman, Ralph Keyes, Mary Boone, and Ralph Mendoza, who in different ways helped make the book a reality. And, of course, I want to thank my family, whose interest and cooperation were a constant source of encouragement.

I feel extremely fortunate and grateful to have had the benefit of the experience and extraordinary talents of Margret McBride as my literary agent and Frederic Hills and Burton Beals as my editors at Simon & Schuster. Working with them has been an education and a genuine pleasure.

Finally, I want to express my deep gratitude to Noel Greenwood, who worked many long days with me here in California to edit and shape the seemingly endless number of drafts of this book. I have grown to be so reliant on his editorial skill, sound judgment, and unflagging good spirits that I certainly would not want to undertake another book without him.

The dissertations by my former students Marcine Johnson and Edith Eger were written for the Saybrook Institute in San Francisco. Some material in the book was adapted from articles of mine that appeared in the *Saturday Review* and the *Journal of Humanistic Psychology*. The chapter "Praising People Does Not Motivate Them" is based on an article I wrote for the *Harvard Business Review*.